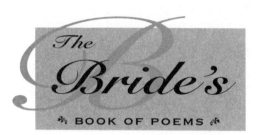

The Bride's

❧ BOOK OF POEMS ❧

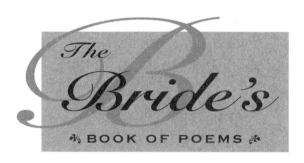

The Bride's

❧ BOOK OF POEMS ❧

CONTEMPORARY
BOOKS
A TRIBUNE NEW MEDIA COMPANY

Library of Congress Cataloging-in-Publication Data

The bride's book of poems / compiled by Cary Yager.
         p.   cm.
      ISBN 0-8092-3439-4 (cloth)
      1. Love poetry.   I. Yager, Cary.
   PN6110.L6B75   1995
   808.81'9354—dc20   94-47951
                                              CIP

Compiled by Cary O. Yager

Published by Contemporary Books, Inc.
Two Prudential Plaza, Chicago, Illinois 60601-6790
Manufactured in the United States of America
International Standard Book Number: 0-8092-3439-4

10   9   8   7   6   5   4   3   2   1

ACKNOWLEDGMENTS

"At a Window," from *Chicago Poems* by Carl
Sandburg. Copyright 1916 by Holt, Rinehart and
Winston, Inc., and renewed 1944 by Carl Sandburg.
Reprinted by permission of Harcourt Brace &
Company.

"Betrothal," from *Selected Poems* by E. J. Scovell.
Copyright 1991 by E. J. Scovell. Reprinted by
permission of Carcanet Press Limited.

"Daybreak," by Stephen Spender. From *Ruins and
Visions* by Stephen Spender. Reprinted by permission
of Faber and Faber Ltd.

"A Dedication," by Alfred, Lord Tennyson. From
The Norton Anthology of English Literature,
courtesy of W. W. Norton & Company, Inc.

"A Dedication to My Wife," by T. S. Eliot. From
The Elder Statesman, copyright © 1959 by Thomas
Stearns Eliot. Copyright renewed 1987 by Valerie
Eliot. This poem also appears in slightly different
form in *Collected Poems 1909–1962* by T. S. Eliot.

The bride hath paced into the hall,
Red as a rose is she.

The Rime of the Ancient Mariner
Samuel Taylor Coleridge (1772–1834)

The Bargain

SIR PHILIP SIDNEY
1554–1586

My true love hath my heart, and I have his,
By just exchange, one for the other given.
I hold his dear, and mine he cannot miss:
There never was a better bargain driven.
His heart in me, keeps me and him in one,
My heart in him, his thoughts and senses
    guides:
He loves my heart, for once it was his own:
I cherish his, because in me it bides.
His heart his wound receivèd from my sight:
My heart was wounded with his wounded
    heart,
For as from me, on him his hurt did light,
So still methought in me his hurt did smart:
    Both equal hurt, in this change sought our
        bliss:
    My true love hath my heart and I have
        his.

My True Love Hath My Heart

CATULLUS

c. 84–c. 54 B.C.

There never was a woman who could say,
    And say it true,
That she was loved of any, O my love,
    As I love you.
There never was a loyal promise given
    Faithful and free,
As loyalty to you, because I love you,
    Is given from me.

A Betrothal

E. J. SCOVELL
1907–

Put your hand on my heart, say that you love
  me as
The woods upon the hills cleave to the hills'
  contours.

I will uphold you, trunk and shoot and
  flowering sheaf,
And I will hold you, roots and fruit and fallen
  leaf.

United

Paulus Silentiarius

How long must we two hide the burning gaze,
And look by stealth in one another's eyes?
Let us proclaim our love; and whoso stays
    The sweet embrace that lulls all miseries—
The sword's our doctor: best that you and I
Should live together, or together die.

TRANSLATED BY W. H. D. ROUSE

Les Estreines

MATTHEW PRIOR
1664–1721

Accept, my love, as true a heart
    As ever lover gave:
'Tis free, it vows, from any art,
    And proud to be your slave.

Then take it kindly, as 'twas meant,
    And let the giver live,
Who, with it, would the world have sent,
    Had it been his to give.

And, that Dorinda may not fear
    I e'er will prove untrue,
My vows shall, ending with the year,
    With it begin anew.

The Passionate Shepherd to His Love

1564–1593

Come live with me and be my love,
And we will all the pleasures prove,
That hills and valleys, dales and fields,
And all the craggy mountains yields.

There we will sit upon the rocks,
And see the shepherds feed their flocks,
By shallow rivers to whose falls
Melodious birds sing madrigals.

And I will make thee beds of roses
With a thousand fragrant posies,
A cap of flowers, and a kirtle
Embroidered all with leaves of myrtle;

A gown made of the finest wool
Which from our pretty lambs we pull;
Fair linèd slippers for the cold,
With buckles of the purest gold;

A belt of straw and ivy buds,
With coral clasps and amber studs:
And if these pleasures may thee move,
Come live with me and be my love.

The shepherds' swains shall dance and sing
For thy delight each May morning:
If these delights thy mind may move,
Then live with me and be my love.

The Happy Swain

AMBROSE PHILIPS
1674–1749

Have ye seen the morning sky,
When the dawn prevails on high,
When, anon, some purply ray
Gives a sample of the day,
When, anon, the lark, on wing,
Strives to soar, and strains to sing?

Have ye seen th'ethereal blue
Gently shedding silvery dew,
Spangling o'er the silent green,
While the nightingale, unseen,
To the moon and stars, full bright,
Lonesome chants the hymn of night?

Have ye seen the broid'red May
All her scented bloom display,
Breezes opening, every hour,
This, and that, expecting flower,
While the mingling birds prolong,
From each bush, the vernal song?

Have ye seen the damask-rose
Her unsully'd blush disclose,
Or the lilly's dewy bell,
In her glossy white, excell,
Or a garden vary'd o'er
With a thousand glories more?

By the beauties these display,
Morning, evening, night, or day
By the pleasures these excite,
Endless sources of delight!
Judge, by them, the joys I find,
Since my Rosalind was kind,
Since she did herself resign
To my vows, for ever mine.

Men Marry What They Need. I Marry You

JOHN CIARDI
1916–1985

Men marry what they need. I marry you,
morning by morning, day by day, night by
    night,
and every marriage makes this marriage new.

In the broken name of heaven, in the light
that shatters granite, by the spitting shore,
in air that leaps and wobbles like a kite,

I marry you from time and a great door
is shut and stays shut against wind, sea, stone,
sunburst, and heavenfall. And home once more

inside our walls of skin and struts of bone,
man-woman, woman-man, and each the other,
I marry you by all dark and all dawn

and learn to let time spend. Why should I
   bother
the flies about me? Let them buzz and do.
Men marry their queen, their daughter, or
   their mother

by names they prove, but that thin buzz
   whines through:
when reason falls to reasons, cause is true.
Men marry what they need. I marry you.

Inclusions

Elizabeth Barrett Browning
1806–1861

Oh, wilt thou have my hand, dear, to lie along
in thine?
As a little stone in a running stream, it seems to
lie and pine.
Now drop the poor pale hand, dear, unfit to
plight with thine.

Oh, wilt thou have my cheek, dear, drawn
closer to thine own?
My cheek is white, my cheek is worn, by many
a tear run down.
Now leave a little space, dear, lest it should wet
thine own.

Oh, must thou have my soul, dear, commingled
with thy soul?
Red grows the cheek, and warm the hand; the
part is in the whole:
Nor hands nor cheeks keep separate, when soul
is joined to soul.

Thou Hast Sworn by Thy God, My Jeanie

ALLAN CUNNINGHAM
1784–1842

Thou hast sworn by thy God, my Jeanie,
  By that pretty white hand o' thine,
And by a' the lowing stars in heaven,
  That thou wad aye by mine!
And I hae sworn by my God, my Jeanie,
  And by that kind heart o' thine,
By a' the stars sown thick owre heaven,
  That thou shalt aye be mine!

The foul fa' the hands that wad loose sic bands,
  And the heart that wad part sic luve!
But there's nae hand can loose the band,
  But the finger o' God abuve.
Though the wee, wee cot maun be my bield,
  An' my claithing ne'er sae mean,
I wad lap me up rich i' the faulds o' luve—
  Heaven's armfu' o' my Jean!

Her white arm wad be a pillow to me,
  Fu' safter than the down;
An' Luve wad winnow owre us his kind, kind
    wings,

An' sweetly I'd sleep, an' soun'.
Come here to me, thou lass, o' my luve!
   Come here and kneel wi' me!
The morn is fu' o' the presence o' God,
   An' I canna pray without thee.

The morn-wind is sweet 'mang the beds o' new
      flowers,
   The wee birds sing kindlie an' hie;
Our gudeman leans owre his kail-yard dike,
   And a blythe auld bodie is he.
The Book maun be ta'en whan the carle come
      hame,
   Wi' the holie psalmodie;
And thou maun speak o' me to thy God,
   And I will speak o' thee.

To Celia

BEN JONSON
1573–1637

Drink to me only with thine eyes,
  And I will pledge with mine;
Or leave a kiss but in the cup
  And I'll not look for wine.
The thirst that from the soul doth rise
  Doth ask a drink divine;
But might I of Jove's nectar sup,
  I would not change for thine.

I sent thee late a rosy wreath,
  Not so much honouring thee
As giving it a hope that there
  It could not withered be;
But thou thereon didst only breathe,
  And sent'st it back to me;
Since when it grows, and smells, I swear,
  Not of itself but thee!

To Cloris

SIR CHARLES SEDLEY
1639–1701

Cloris, I cannot say your eyes
Did my unwary heart surprise;
Nor will I swear it was your face,
Your shape, or any nameless grace:
For you are so entirely fair,
To love a part, injustice were;
No drowning man can know which drop
Of water his last breath did stop;
So when the stars in heaven appear,
And join to make the night look clear;
The light we no one's bounty call,
But the obliging gift of all.
He that does lips or hands adore,
Deserves them only, and no more;
But I love all, and every part,
And nothing less can ease my heart.
Cupid, that lover, weakly strikes,
Who can express what 'tis he likes.

To F. C.

20th February 1875

MORTIMER COLLINS
1827–1876

Fast falls the snow, O lady mine,
Sprinkling the lawn with crystals fine,
But by the gods we won't repine
    While we're together,
We'll chat and rhyme and kiss and dine,
    Defying weather.

So stir the fire and pour the wine,
And let those sea-green eyes divine
Pour their love-madness into mine:
    I don't care whether
'Tis snow or sun or rain or shine
    If we're together.

Sweet Mouth,
That Send'st a Musky-Rosed Breath

JOSHUA SYLVESTER

1563–1618

Sweet mouth, that send'st a musky-rosed breath;
Fountain of nectar and delightful balm;
Eyes cloudy-clear, smile-frowning, stormy-calm;
Whose every glance darts me a living-death
Brows, bending quaintly your round ebene arks;
Smile, that than Venus sooner Mars besots;
Locks more than golden, curl'd in curious knots,
Where, in close ambush, wanton Cupid lurks;
Grace Angel-like; fair fore-head, smooth, and
   high;
Pure white, that dimm'st the lilies of the vale;
Vermilion rose, that mak'st Aurora pale:
Rare spirit, to rule this beautious Emperie:
     If in your force, divine effects I view,
     Ah, who can blame me, if I worship you?

Love Not Me for Comely Grace

ANONYMOUS

Love not me for comely grace,
For my pleasing eye or face,
Nor for any outward part,
No, nor for my constant heart;
   For those may fail or turn to ill,
     So thou and I shall sever;
Keep therefore a true woman's eye,
And love me still, but know not why.
   So hast thou the same reason still
     To dote upon me ever.

If Thou Must Love Me, Let It Be for Nought

Elizabeth Barrett Browning
1806–1861

If thou must love me, let it be for nought
Except for love's sake only. Do not say
"I love her for her smile . . . her look . . . her
    way
Of speaking gently . . . for a trick of thought
That falls in well with mine, and certes brought
A sense of pleasant ease on such a day" —
For these things in themselves beloved, may
Be changed, or change for thee — and love, so
    wrought
May be unwrought so. Neither love me for
Thine own dear pity's wiping my cheeks dry —
A creature might forget to weep, who bore
Thy comfort long, and lose thy love thereby!
But love me for love's sake, that evermore
Thou may'st love on, through love's eternity.

Seeing Her Dancing

ROBERT HEATH
fl. 1650

Robes loosely flowing and aspect as free,
A careless carriage decked with modesty;
   A smiling look, but yet severe:
   Such comely graces about her were.

Her steps with such an evenness she wove
As she could hardly be perceived to move;
   Whilst, her silk sails displayèd, she
   Swam like a ship with majesty.

As when with steadfast eyes we view the sun
We know it goes though see no motion;
   So undiscerned she moved, that we
   Perceived she stirred, but did not see.

At a Window

CARL SANDBURG
1878–1967

Give me hunger,
O you gods that sit and give
The world its orders.
Give me hunger, pain and want,
Shut me out with shame and failure
From your doors of gold and fame,
Give me your shabbiest, weariest hunger!

But leave me a little love,
A voice to speak to me in the day end,
A hand to touch me in the dark room
Breaking the long loneliness.
In the dusk of day-shapes
Blurring the sunset,
One little wandering, western star
Thrust out from the changing shores of shadow.
Let me go to the window,
Watch there the day-shapes of dusk
And wait and know the coming
Of a little love.

Live in My Heart and Pay No Rent

Samuel Lover
1787–1868

'Vourneen, when your days were bright,
Never an eye did I dare to lift to you,
But now, in your fortune's blight,
False ones are flying in sunshine that knew you;
　But still on one welcome true rely,
　Tho' the crops may fail, and the cow go dry,
And your cabin be burned, and all be spent,
Come, live in my heart and pay no rent;
　Come, come, live in my heart,
Live in my heart and pay no rent;
　Come, come, live in my heart,
Live in my heart, mavourneen!

'Vourneen, dry up those tears,
The sensible people will tell you to wait, dear,
But ah! in the wasting of Love's young years,
On our innocent hearts we're committing a
    chate, dear.
    For hearts when they're young should make
      the vow,
    For when they are old they don't know how;
So marry at once and you'll not repent,
When you live in my heart and pay no rent,
    Come, come, live in my heart,
Live in my heart and pay no rent,
    Come, come, live in my heart,
Live in my heart, mavourneen!

First Love

JOHN CLARE
1793–1864

I ne'er was struck before that hour
    With love so sudden and so sweet,
Her face it bloomed like a sweet flower
    And stole my heart away complete.

My face turned pale as deadly pale,
    My legs refused to walk away,
And when she looked, what could I ail?
    My life and all seemed turned to clay.

And then my blood rushed to my face
    And took my eyesight quite away,
The trees and bushes round the place
    Seemed midnight at noonday.
I could not see a single thing,
    Words from my eyes did start—
They spoke as chords do from the string,
    And blood burnt round my heart.

Are flowers the winter's choice?
  Is love's bed always snow?
She seemed to hear my silent voice,
  Not love's appeals to know.
I never saw so sweet a face
  As that I stood before.
My heart has left its dwelling-place
  And can return no more.

A Match

ALGERNON CHARLES SWINBURNE
1837–1909

If love were what the rose is,
 And I were like the leaf,
Our lives would grow together
In sad or singing weather,
Blown fields or flowerful closes,
 Green pleasure or grey grief;
If love were what the rose is,
 And I were like the leaf.

If I were what the words are,
 And love were like the tune,
With double sound and single
Delight our lips would mingle,
With kisses glad as birds are
 That get sweet rain at noon;
If I were what the words are,
 And love were like the tune.

If you were life, my darling,
 And I your love were death,
We'd shine and snow together
Ere March made sweet the weather

With daffodil and starling
    And hours of fruitful breath;
If you were life, my darling,
    And I your love were death.

If you were thrall to sorrow,
    And I were page to joy,
We'd play for lives and seasons
With loving looks and treasons
And tears of night and morrow
    And laughs of maid and boy;
If you were thrall to sorrow,
    And I were page to joy.

If you were April's lady,
    And I were lord in May,
We'd throw with leaves for hours
And draw for days with flowers,
Till day like night were shady
    And night were bright like day;
If you were April's lady,
    And I were lord in May.

If you were queen of pleasure,
  And I were king of pain,
We'd hunt down love together,
Pluck out his flying-feather,
And teach his feet a measure,
  And find his mouth a rein;
If you were queen of pleasure,
  And I were king of pain.

Lochinvar

SIR WALTER SCOTT
1771–1832

O, young Lochinvar is come out of the west,
Through all the wide Border his steed was the
    best;
And save his good broadsword he weapons had
    none,
He rode all unarmed, and he rode all alone.
So faithful in love, and so dauntless in war,
There never was knight like the young
    Lochinvar.

He stayed not for brake, and he stopped not for
    stone,
He swam the Eske river where ford there was
    none;
But ere he alighted at Netherby gate,
The bride had consented, the gallant came late:
For a laggard in love, and a dastard in war,
Was to wed the fair Ellen of brave Lochinvar.

So boldly he entered the Netherby Hall,
Among bride's-men, and kinsmen, and brothers,
    and all:

Then spoke the bride's father, his hand on his
  sword,
(For the poor craven bridegroom said never a
  word)
'O come ye in peace here, or come ye in war,
Or to dance at our bridal, young Lord
  Lochinvar?'

'I long wooed your daughter, my suit you
  denied;—
Love swells like the Solway, but ebbs like its
  tide—
And now am I come, with this lost love of
  mine,
To lead but one measure, drink one cup of
  wine.
There are maidens in Scotland more lovely by
  far,
That would gladly be bride to the young
  Lochinvar.'

The bride kissed the goblet: the knight took it
  up,
He quaffed off the wine, and he threw down
  the cup.
She looked down to blush, and she looked up to
  sigh,
With a smile on her lips, and a tear in her eye.

He took her soft hand, ere her mother could
    bar,—
'Now tread we a measure!' said the young
    Lochinvar.

So stately his form and so lovely her face,
That never a hall such a galliard did grace;
While her mother did fret, and her father did
    fume,
And the bridegroom stood dangling his bonnet
    and plume;
And the bride-maidens whispered, ' 'Twere
    better by far,
To have matched our fair cousin with young
    Lochinvar.'

One touch to her hand, and one word in her
    ear,
When they reached the hall-door, and the
    charger stood near;
So light to the croup the fair lady he swung,
So light to the saddle before her he sprung!
'She is won! we are gone, over bank, bush, and
    scaur;
They'll have fleet steeds that follow,' quoth
    young Lochinvar.

There was mounting 'mong Graemes of the
  Netherby clan;
Forsters, Fenwicks, and Musgraves, they rode
  and they ran:
There was racing and chasing on Cannobie
  Lee,
But the lost bride of Netherby ne'er did they
  see.
So daring in love, and so dauntless in war,
Have ye e'er heard of gallant like young
  Lochinvar?

From "Love in the Valley"

GEORGE MEREDITH
1828–1909

Under yonder beech-tree standing on the green
　　swa rd,
Couched with her arms behind her little head,
Her knees folded up, and her tresses on her
　　bosom,
Lies my young love sleeping in the shade.
Had I the heart to slide one arm beneath her!
Press her dreaming lips as her waist I folded
　　slow,
Waking on the instant she could not but
　　embrace me—
Ah! would she hold me, and never let me go?

· · ·

When her mother tends her before the
　　laughing mirror,
Tying up her laces, looping up her hair,
Often she thinks—were this wild thing wedded,
I should have more love, and much less care.
When her mother tends her before the bashful
　　mirror,
Loosening her laces, combing down her curls,
Often she thinks—were this wild thing wedded,
I should lose but one for so many boys and
　　girls.

Comes a sudden question—should a strange
    hand pluck her!
Oh! what an anguish smites me at the thought!
Should some idle lordling bribe her mind with
    jewels!
Can such beauty ever thus be bought?
Sometimes the huntsmen, prancing down the
    valley,
Eye the village lasses, full of sprightly mirth;
They see, as I see, mine is the fairest!
Would she were older and could read my
    worth!

. . .

When at dawn she wakens, and her fair face
    gazes
Out on the weather through the window panes,
Beauteous she looks! like a white water-lily
Bursting out of bud on the rippled river plains.
When from bed she rises, clothed from neck to
    ankle
In her long night gown, sweet as boughs of
    May,
Beauteous she looks! like a tall garden lily,
Pure from the night and perfect for the day!

. . .

Shall the birds in vain then valentine their
    sweethearts?
Season after season tell a fruitless tale?
Will not the virgin listen to their voices?

Take the honeyed meaning, wear the bridal
    veil?
Fears she frosts of winter, fears she the bare
    branches?
Waits she the garlands of spring for her dower?
Is she a nightingale that will not be nested
Till the April woodland has built her bridal
    bower?

Then come, merry April, with all thy birds
    and beauties!
With thy crescent brows and thy flowery,
    showery glee;
With thy budding leafage and fresh green
    pastures;
And may thy lustrous crescent grow a
    honeymoon for me!
Come, merry month of the cuckoo and the
    violet!
Come, weeping loveliness in all thy blue delight!
Lo! the nest is ready, let me not languish longer!
Bring her to my arms on the first May night.

Cooking and Courting

ANONYMOUS

From Tom to Ned

Dear Ned, no doubt you'll be surprised
    When you receive and read this letter.
I've railed against the marriage state;
    But then, you see, I knew no better.
I've met a lovely girl out here;
    Her manner is—well—very winning:
We're soon to be—well, Ned, my dear,
    I'll tell you all, from the beginning.

I went to ask her out to ride
    Last Wednesday—it was perfect weather.
She said she couldn't possibly:
    The servants had gone off together
(Hibernians always rush away,
    At cousins' funerals to be looking);
Pies must be made, and she must stay,
    She said, to do that branch of cooking.

"O, let me help you," then I cried:
    "I'll be a cooker too—how jolly!"
She laughed, and answered, with a smile,
    "All right! but you'll repent your folly;

For I shall be a tyrant, sir,
  And good hard work you'll have to grapple;
So sit down there, and don't you stir,
  But take this knife, and pare that apple."

She rolled her sleeve above her arm,—
  That lovely arm, so plump and rounded;
Outside, the morning sun shone bright;
  Inside, the dough she deftly pounded.
Her little fingers sprinkled flour,
  And rolled the pie-crust up in masses:
I passed the most delightful hour
  Mid butter, sugar, and molasses.

With deep reflection her sweet eyes
  Gazed on each pot and pan and kettle.
She sliced the apples, filled her pies,
  And then the upper crust did settle.
Her rippling waves of golden hair
  In one great coil were tightly twisted;
But locks would break it, here and there,
  And curl about where'er they listed.

And then her sleeve came down, and I
  Fastened it up—her hands were doughy;
O, it did take the longest time!—
  Her arm, Ned, was so round and snowy.
She blushed, and trembled, and looked shy;
  Somehow that made me all the bolder;
Her arch lips looked so red that I—
  Well—found her head upon my shoulder.

We're to be married, Ned, next month;
    Come and attend the wedding revels.
I really think that bachelors
    Are the most miserable devils!
You'd better go for some girl's hand;
    And if you are uncertain whether
You dare to make a due demand,
    Why, just try cooking pies together.

The Exchange

SAMUEL TAYLOR COLERIDGE
1772–1834

We pledged our hearts, my love and I,
    I in my arms the maiden clasping;
I could not tell the reason why,
    But, O, I trembled like an aspen!

Her father's love she bade me gain;
    I went, and shook like any reed!
I strove to act the man—in vain!
    We had exchanged our hearts indeed.

The Wedding Gift

MINNA IRVING
1872–?

In the garret under the sloping eaves
    Stood Grandmother Granger's old hair trunk,
With battered bureaus and broken chairs,
    And a spinning wheel and similar junk.
The hirsute cover was worn in spots;
    'Twas once the hide of a brindle cow,
That grazed of yore in the meadows green
    Where Harlem flats are towering now.

I used to climb the garret stairs
    On a rainy day and lift the lid
And loose the fragrance of olden times
    That under the faded finery hid—
Damask roses and lavender,
    Delicate odors, fine and faint,
Clinging still to the crumpled folds
    Of silks and muslins and challies quaint.

Fans and slippers and veils were there,
    Beads of amber and yellow lace,
Coral earrings and Paisley shawls,
    And the big pink bonnet that framed her
        face

With its golden curls and soft blue eyes,
    And the dimpled chin and the laughing lip,
When Grandfather Granger took his bride
    And the smart new trunk on a wedding trip.

It was the soul of a garden old,
    Dreaming under the stars, I freed.
Jasmine, lilies, and rosemary,
    Stately marigolds gone to seed.
Thyme and pansy and mignonette,
    Sage and balsam and love-in-a-mist,
Where Grandfather Granger, a bold young
        blade,
    Scaled the walls to the secret tryst.

To the creak and sway of a four-horse stage
    He kissed her hand in its silken mitt,
And her girlish cheek that was like a rose
    As her blissful blushes mantled it.
The honeymoon never waned, they say—
    The pair were lovers through all the years,
Gray-haired sweethearts, tender and true,
    Sharing life with its smiles and tears.

The flowery frocks and the ancient trunk,
    And Grandmother Granger, too, are dust,
But something precious and sweet and rare
    Survives the havoc of moth and rust;
Love with the wings of bright romance,
    And the eyes of youth that are always gay—
Grandmother Granger's wedding gift
    To every girl on her marriage day.

A Maiden's Ideal of a Husband
from "The Contrivances"

HENRY CAREY
c. 1687–1743

Genteel in personage,
Conduct, and equipage,
Noble by heritage,
  Generous and free:
Brave, not romantic;
Learned, not pedantic;
Frolic, not frantic;
  This must he be.
Honor maintaining,
Meanness disdaining,
Still entertaining,
  Engaging and new.
Neat, but not finical;
Sage, but not cynical;
Never tyrannical,
  But ever true.

Song *from* "The Witch"

THOMAS MIDDLETON
1570?–1627

In a maiden-time professed,
Then we say that life is best;
Tasting once the married life,
Then we only praise the wife;
There's but one state more to try
Which makes women laugh or cry—
Widow, widow. Of these three
The middle's best, and that give me.

Ballad Written for a Bridegroom

FRANCOIS VILLON
1431–?

At daybreak, when the falcon claps his wings,
  No whit for grief, but noble heart and high
With loud glad noise he stirs himself and
      springs,
    And takes his meat and toward his lure
      draws nigh;
    Such good I wish you! Yea, and heartily
I am fired with hope of true love's meed to get;
    Know that Love writes it in his book; for
      why,
This is the end for which we twain are met.

Mine own heart's lady with no gainsayings
  You shall be always wholly till I die;
And in my right against all bitter things
    Sweet laurel with fresh rose its force shall
      try;
    Seeing reason wills not that I cast love by
(Nor here with reason shall I chide or fret)
    Nor cease to serve, but serve more constantly;
This is the end for which we twain are met.

And, which is more, when grief about me clings
　　Through Fortune's fit or fume of jealousy,
Your sweet kind eye beats down her
　　　threatenings
　　As wind doth smoke; such power sits in your
　　　eye.
　　Thus in your field my seed of harvestry
Thrives, for the fruit is like me that I set;
　　God bids me tend it with good husbandry;
This is the end for which we twain are met.

Princess, give ear to this my summary;
　　That heart of mine your heart's love should
　　　forget,
Shall never be: like trust in you put I:
　　This is the end for which we twain are met.

TRANSLATED BY ALGERNON CHARLES SWINBURNE

From "Prothalamion"

EDMUND SPENSER
1552?–1599

Calm was the day, and through the trembling
    air
Sweet-breathing Zephyrus did softly play
A gentle spirit, that lightly did delay
Hot Titan's beams, which then did glister fair;
When I, (whom sullen care,
Through discontent of my long fruitless stay
In Prince's Court, and expectation vain
Of idle hopes, which still do fly away,
Like empty shadows, did afflict my brain,)
Walked forth to ease my pain
Along the shore of silver streaming Thames;
Whose rutty bank, the which his river hems,
Was painted all with variable flowers,
And all the meads adorned with dainty gems
Fit to deck maidens' bowers,
And crown their paramours
Against the bridal day, which is not long:
    Sweet Thames! run softly, till I end my song.

There, in a meadow, by the river's side,
A flock of nymphs I chancèd to espy,
All lovely daughters of the flood thereby,

With goodly greenish locks, all loose untied,
As each had been a bride;
And each one had a little wicker basket,
Made of the twigs, entrailèd curiously,
In which they gathered flowers to fill their
    flasket,
And with fine fingers cropt full feateously
The tender stalks on high.
Of every sort, which in that meadow grew,
They gathered some; the violet, pallid blue,
The little daisy, that at evening closes,
The virgin lily, and the primrose true,
With store of vermeil roses,
To deck their bridegrooms' posies
Against the bridal day, which was not long:
    Sweet Thames! run softly, till I end my song.

With that I saw two swans of goodly hue
Come softly swimming down along the lea;
Two fairer birds I yet did never see;
The snow, which doth the top of Pindus strew,
Did never whiter show;
Nor Jove himself, when he a swan would be
For love of Leda, whiter did appear;
Yet Leda was (they say) as white as he,
Yet not so white as these, nor nothing near;
So purely white they were,
That even the gentle stream, the which them
    bare,
Seemed foul to them, and bade his billows spare

To wet their silken feathers, lest they might
Soil their fair plumes with water not so fair,
And mar their beauties bright,
That shone as heaven's light,
Against their bridal day, which was not long:
    Sweet Thames! run softly, till I end my song.

. . .

"Ye gentle birds! the world's fair ornament,
And heaven's glory, whom this happy hour
Doth lead unto your lovers' blissful bower,
Joy may you have, and gentle heart's content
Of your love's couplement;
And let fair Venus, that is queen of love,
With her heart-quelling son upon you smile,
Whose smile, they say, hath virtue to remove
All Love's dislike, and friendship's faulty guile
For ever to assoil.
Let endless Peace your steadfast hearts accord,
And blessèd Plenty wait upon your board;
And let your bed with pleasures chaste abound,
That fruitful issue may to you afford,
Which may your foes confound,
And make your joys redound
Upon your bridal day, which is not long:
    Sweet Thames! run softly, till I end my
    song."

Epithalamion

EDMUND SPENSER
1552?–1599

Ye learned sisters which have oftentimes
Beene to me ayding, others to adorne:
Whom ye thought worthy of your gracefull
    rymes,
That even the greatest did not greatly scorne
To heare theyr names sung in your simple
    layes,
But joyed in theyr prayse.
And when ye list your owne mishaps to
    mourne,
Which death, or love, or fortunes wreck did
    rayse,
Your string could soone to sadder tenor turne,
And teach the woods and waters to lament
Your dolefull dreriment.
Now lay those sorrowfull complaints aside,
And having all your heads with girland crownd,
Helpe me mine owne loves prayses to resound,
Ne let the same of any be envide
So Orpheus did for his owne bride,
So I unto my selfe alone will sing,
The woods shall to me answer and my Eccho
    ring.

Early before the worlds light giving lampe,
His golden beame upon the hils doth spred,
Having disperst the nights unchearefull dampe,
Doe ye awake, and with fresh lusty hed,
Go to the bowre of my beloved love,
My truest turtle dove,
Bid her awake; for Hymen is awake,
And long since ready forth his maske to move,
With his bright Tead that flames with many a
    flake,
And many a bachelor to waite on him,
In theyr fresh garments trim.
Bid her awake therefore and soone her dight,
For lo the wished day is come at last,
That shall for al the paynes and sorrowes past,
Pay to her usury of long delight:
And whylest she doth her dight,
Doe ye to her of joy and solace sing,
That all the woods may answer and your eccho
    ring.

Bring with you all the Nymphes that you can
    heare
Both of the rivers and the forrests greene:
And of the sea that neighbours to her neare,
Al with gay girlands goodly wel beseene.
And let them also with them bring in hand,
Another gay girland
For my fayre love of lillyes and of roses,
Bound truelove wize with a blew silke riband.

And let them make great store of bridale poses,
And let them eeke bring store of other flowers
To deck the bridale bowers.
And let the ground whereas her foot shall
    tread,
For feare the stones her tender foot should
    wrong
Be strewed with fragrant flowers all along,
And diapred lyke the discolored mead.
Which done, doe at her chamber dore awayt,
For she will waken strayt,
The whiles doe ye this song unto her sing,
The woods shall to you answer and your Eccho
    ring.

Ye Nymphes of Mulla which with carefull
    heed,
The silver scaly trouts doe tend full well,
And greedy pikes which use therein to feed,
(Those trouts and pikes all others doo excell)
And ye likewise which keepe the rushy lake,
Where none doo fishes take,
Bynd up the locks the which hang scatterd
    light,
And in his waters which your mirror make,
Behold your faces as the christall bright,
That when you come whereas my love doth lie,
No blemish she may spie.
And eke ye lightfoot mayds which keepe the
    deere,

That on the hoary mountayne use to towre,
And the wylde wolves which seeke them to
    devoure,
With your steele darts doo chace from
    comming neer
Be also present heere,
To helpe to decke her and to help to sing,
That all the woods may answer and your eccho
    ring.

Wake now, my love, awake; for it is time.
The Rosy Morne long since left Tithones bed,
All ready to her silver coche to clyme,
And Phoebus gins to shew his glorious hed.
Hark how the cheerefull birds do chaunt theyr
    laies
And carroll of loves praise.
The merry Larke hir mattins sings aloft,
The thrush replyes, the Mavis descant playes,
The Ouzell shrills, the Ruddock warbles soft,
So goodly all agree with sweet consent,
To this dayes merriment.
Ah my deere love, why doe ye sleepe thus long,
When meeter were that ye should now awake,
T'awayt the comming of your joyous make,
And hearken to the birds lovelearned song,
The deawy leaves among.
For they of joy and pleasance to you sing,
That all the woods them answer and theyr
    eccho ring.

My love is now awake out of her dreame,
And her fayre eyes, like stars that dimmed were
With darksome cloud, now shew theyr goodly
   beams
More bright then Hesperus his head doth rere.
Come now, ye damzels, daughters of delight,
Helpe quickly her to dight,
But first come, ye fayre houres which were
   begot
In Joves sweet paradice, of Day and Night,
Which doe the seasons of the yeare allot,
And al that ever in this world is fayre
Doe make and still repayre.
And ye three handmayds of the Cyprian
   Queene,
The which doe still adorne her beauties pride,
Helpe to addorne my beautifullest bride:
And as ye her array, still throw betweene
Some graces to be seene,
And as ye use to Venus, to her sing,
The whiles the woods shal answer and your
   eccho ring.

Now is my love all ready forth to come;
Let all the virgins therefore well awayt,
And ye fresh boyes that tend upon her groome
Prepare your selves; for he is comming strayt.
Set all your things in seemely good aray
Fit for so joyfull day,
The joyfulst day that ever sunne did see.

Faire Sun, shew forth thy favourable ray,
And let thy lifull heat not fervent be
For feare of burning her sunshyny face,
Her beauty to disgrace.
O fayrest Phoebus, father of the Muse,
If ever I did honour thee aright,
Or sing the thing, that mote thy mind delight,
Doe not thy servants simple boone refuse,
But let this day, let this one day, be myne,
Let all the rest be thine.
Then I thy soverayne prayses loud wil sing,
That all the woods shal answer and theyr eccho
    ring.

Harke how the Minstrels gin to shrill aloud
Their merry Musick that resounds from far,
The pipe, the tabor, and the trembling Croud,
That well agree withouten breach or jar.
But most of all the Damzels doe delite,
When they their tymbrels smyte,
And thereunto doe daunce and carrol sweet,
That all the sences they doe ravish quite,
The whyles the boyes run up and downe the
    street,
Crying aloud with strong confused noyce,
As if it were one voyce.
Hymen, io, Hymen, Hymen, they do shout,
That even to the heavens theyr shouting shrill
Doth reach, and all the firmament doth fill,
To which the people standing all about,

As in approvance doe thereto applaud
And loud advance her laud,
And evermore they Hymen, Hymen sing,
That al the woods should answer and your echo
   ring.

Open the temple gates unto my love,
Open them wide that she may enter in,
Arysing forth to run her mighty race,
Clad all in white, that seemes a virgin best.
So well it her beseemes that ye would weene
Some angell she had beene.
Her long loose yellow locks lyke golden wyre,
Sprinckled with perle, and perling flowres a
   tweene,
Doe lyke a golden mantle her attyre,
And being crowned with a girland greene,
Seeme lyke some mayden Queene.
Her modest eyes abashed to behold
So many gazers, as on her do stare,
Upon the lowly ground affixed are.
Ne dare lift up her countenance too bold,
But blush to heare her prayses sung so loud,
So farre from being proud.
Nathlesse doe ye still loud her prayses sing.
That all the woods may answer and your eccho
   ring.

Tell me, ye merchants daughters, did ye see
So fayre a creature in your towne before,
So sweet, so lovely, and so mild as she,

Adornd with beautyes grace and vertues store,
Her goodly eyes lyke Saphyres shining bright,
Her forehead yvory white,
Her cheekes lyke apples which the sun hath
    rudded,
Her lips lyke cherryes charming men to byte,
Her brest like to a bowle of creame uncrudded,
Her paps lyke lyllies budded,
Her snowie necke lyke to a marble towre,
And all her body like a pallace fayre,
Ascending uppe with many a stately stayre,
To honors seat and chastities sweet bowre.
Why stand ye still, ye virgins, in amaze,
Upon her so to gaze,
Whiles ye forget your former lay to sing,
To which the woods did answer and your eccho
    ring.

But if ye saw that which no eyes can see,
The inward beauty of her lively spright,
Garnisht with heavenly guifts of high degree,
Much more then would ye wonder at that sight,
And stand astonisht lyke to those which red
Medusaes mazeful hed.
There dwels sweet love and constant chastity,
Unspotted fayth and comely womanhood,
Regard of honour and mild modesty,
There vertue raynes as Queene in royal
    throne,
And giveth lawes alone.

The which the base affections doe obay,
And yeeld theyr services unto her will,
Ne thought of thing uncomely ever may
Thereto approch to tempt her mind to ill.
Had ye once seene these her celestial threasures,
And unrevealed pleasures,
Then would ye wonder and her prayses sing,
That al the woods should answer and your
    eccho ring.

Open the temple gates unto my love,
Open them wide that she may enter in,
And all the postes adorne as doth behove,
And all the pillours deck with girlands trim,
For to recyve this Saynt with honour dew,
That commeth in to you.
With trembling steps and humble reverence,
She commeth in, before th'almighties vew,
Of her, ye virgins, learne obedience,
When so ye come into those holy places,
To humble your proud faces:
Bring her up to th'high altar, that she may
The sacred ceremonies there partake,
The which do endlesse matrimony make,
And let the roring Organs loudly play
The praises of the Lord in lively notes,
The whiles with hollow throates
The Choristers the joyous Antheme sing,
That al the woods may answere and their eccho
    ring.

Behold whiles she before the altar stands
Hearing the holy priest that to her speakes
And blesseth her with his two happy hands,
How the red roses flush up in her cheekes,
And the pure snow with goodly vermill stayne,
Like crimsin dyde in grayne,
That even th'Angels which continually
About the sacred Altare doe remaine,
Forget their service and about her fly,
Ofte peeping in her face that seemes more
    fayre,
The more they on it stare.
But her sad eyes still fastened on the ground,
Are governed with goodly modesty,
That suffers not one looke to glaunce awry,
Which may let in a little thought unsownd.
Why blush ye, love, to give to me your hand,
The pledge of all our band?
Sing ye, sweet Angels, Alleluya sing,
That all the woods may answere and your
    eccho ring.

Now al is done; bring home the bride againe,
Bring home the triumph of our victory,
Bring home with you the glory of her gaine,
With joyance bring her and with jollity.
Never had man more joyfull day then this,
Whom heaven would heape with blis.
Make feast therefore now all this live long day,
This day for ever to me holy is,

Poure out the wine without restraint or stay,
Poure not by cups, but by the belly full,
Poure out to all that wull,
And sprinkle all the postes and wals with wine,
That they may sweat, and drunken be withall.
Crowne ye God Bacchus with a coronall,
And Hymen also crowne with wreathes of vine,
And let the Graces daunce unto the rest;
For they can doo it best:
The whiles the maydens doe theyr carroll sing,
To which the woods shal answer and theyr
    eccho ring.

Ring ye the bels, ye yong men of the towne,
And leave your wonted labors for this day:
This day is holy; doe ye write it downe,
That ye for ever it remember may.
This day the sunne is in his chiefest hight,
With Barnaby the bright,
From whence declining daily by degrees,
He somewhat loseth of his heat and light,
When once the Crab behind his back he sees.
But for this time it ill ordained was,
To chose the longest day in all the yeare,
And shortest night, when longest fitter weare:
Yet never day so long, but late would passe.
Ring ye the bels, to make it weare away,
And bonefiers make all day,
And daunce about them, and about them sing,
That all the woods may answer, and your eccho
    ring.

Ah when will this long weary day have end,
And lende me leave to come unto my love?
How slowly do the houres theyr numbers
    spend!
How slowly does sad Time his feathers move!
Hast thee, O fayrest Planet, to thy home
Within the Western fome:
Thy tyred steedes long since have need of rest.
Long though it be, at last I see it gloome,
And the bright evening star with golden creast
Appeare out of the East.
Fayre childe of beauty, glorious lampe of love,
That all the host of heaven in rankes doost
    lead,
And guydest lovers through the nightes dread,
How chearefully thou lookest from above,
And seemst to laugh atweene thy twinkling light
As joying in the sight
Of these glad many which for joy doe sing,
That all the woods them answer and their echo
    ring.

Now ceasse, ye damsels, your delights forepast;
Enough is it, that all the day was youres:
Now day is doen, and night is nighing fast:
Now bring the Bryde into the brydall boures.
Now night is come, now soone her disaray,
And in her bed her lay;
Lay her in lillies and in violets,
And silken courteins over her display,
And odourd sheetes, and Arras coverlets.

Behold how goodly my faire love does ly
In proud humility;
Like unto Maia, when as Jove her tooke,
In Tempe, lying on the flowry gras,
Twixt sleepe and wake, after she weary was,
With bathing in the Acidalian brooke.
Now it is night, ye damsels may be gon,
And leave my love alone,
And leave likewise your former lay to sing:
The woods no more shal answere, nor your
    echo ring.

Now welcome night, thou night so long
    expected,
That long daies labour doest at last defray,
And all my cares, which cruell love collected,
Hast sumd in one, and cancelled for aye:
Spread thy broad wing over my love and me,
That no man may us see,
And in thy sable mantle us enwrap,
From feare of perill and foule horror free.
Let no false treason seeke us to entrap,
Nor any dread disquiet once annoy
The safety of our joy:
But let the night be calme and quietsome,
Without tempestuous storms or sad afray:
Lyke as when Jove with fayre Alcmena lay,
When he begot the great Tirynthian groome:
Or lyke as when he with thy selfe did lie,
And begot Majesty.

And let the mayds and yongmen cease to sing:
Ne let the woods them answer, nor theyr eccho
ring.

Let no lamenting cryes, nor dolefull teares,
Be heard all night within nor yet without:
Ne let false whispers, breeding hidden feares,
Breake gentle sleepe with misconceived dout.
Let no deluding dreames, nor dreadful sights
Make sudden sad affrights;
Ne let housefyres, nor lightnings helpelesse
harmes,
Ne let the Pouke, nor other evill sprights,
Ne let mischivous witches with theyr charmes,
Ne let hob Goblins, names whose sence we see
not,
Fray us with things that be not.
Let not the shriech Oule, nor the Storke be
heard,
Nor the night Raven that still deadly yels,
Nor damned ghosts cald up with mighty spels,
Nor griesly vultures make us once affeard,
Ne let th'unpleasant Quyre of Frogs still
croking
Make us to wish theyr choking.
Let none of these theyr drery accents sing;
Ne let the woods them answer, nor theyr eccho
ring.

But let stil Silence trew night watches keepe,
That sacred peace may in assurance rayne,

And tymely sleep, when it is tyme to sleepe,
May poure his limbs forth on your pleasant
   playne,
The whiles an hundred little winged loves,
Like divers fethered doves,
Shall fly and flutter round about your bed,
And in the secret darke, that none reproves,
Their prety stealthes shal worke, and snares
   shal spread
To filch away sweet snatches of delight,
Conceald through covert night.
Ye sonnes of Venus, play your sports at will,
For greedy pleasure, carelesse of your toyes,
Thinks more upon her paradise of joyes,
Then what ye do, albe it good or ill.
All night therefore attend your merry play,
For it will soone be day:
Now none doth hinder you, that say or sing,
Ne will the woods now answer, nor your Eccho
   ring.

Who is the same, which at my window peepes?
Or whose is that faire face, that shines so
   bright,
Is it not Cinthia, she that never sleepes,
But walkes about high heaven al the night?
O fayrest goddesse, do thou not envy
My love with me to spy:
For thou likewise didst love, though now
   unthought,

And for a fleece of woll, which privily
The Latmian shephard once unto thee brought,
His pleasures with thee wrought.
Therefore to us be favorable now;
And sith of wemens labours thou hast charge,
And generation goodly dost enlarge,
Encline thy will t'effect our wishfull vow,
And the chast wombe informe with timely seed,
That may our comfort breed:
Till which we cease our hopefull hap to sing,
Ne let the woods us answere, nor our Eccho
    ring.

And thou, great Juno, which with awful might
The lawes of wedlock still dost patronize,
And the religion of the faith first plight
With sacred rites hast taught to solemnize:
And eeke for comfort often called art
Of women in their smart,
Eternally bind thou this lovely band,
And all thy blessings unto us impart.
And thou, glad Genius, in whose gentle hand
The bridale bowre and geniall bed remaine,
Without blemish or staine,
And the sweet pleasures of theyr loves delight
With secret ayde doest succour and supply,
Till they bring forth the fruitfull progeny,
Send us the timely fruit of this same night.

And thou, fayre Hebe, and thou, Hymen free,
Grant that it may so be.
Til which we cease your further prayse to sing,
Ne any woods shal answer, nor your Eccho
   ring.

And ye high heavens, the temple of the gods,
In which a thousand torches flaming bright
Doe burne, that to us wretched earthly clods
In dreadful darknesse lend desired light;
And all ye powers which in the same remayne,
More then we men can fayne,
Poure out your blessing on us plentiously
And happy influence upon us raine,
That we may raise a large posterity,
Which from the earth, which they may long
   possesse,
With lasting happinesse,
Up to your haughty pallaces may mount,
And for the guerdon of theyr glorious merit
May heavenly tabernacles there inherit,
Of blessed Saints for to increase the count.
So let us rest, sweet love, in hope of this,
And cease till then our tymely joyes to sing,
The woods no more us answer, nor our eccho
   ring.

Song, made in lieu of many ornaments,
With which my love should duly have bene
   dect,

Which cutting off through hasty accidents,
Ye would not stay your dew time to expect,
But promist both to recompens,
Be unto her a goodly ornament,
And for short time an endlesse moniment.

Adam Describing Eve
from "Paradise Lost, Book VIII"

JOHN MILTON
1608–1674

Mine eyes he closed, but open left the cell
Of fancy, my internal sight, by which
Abstract, as in a trance, methought I saw,
Though sleeping, where I lay, and saw the
    shape
Still glorious before whom awake I stood;
Who, stooping, opened my left side, and took
From thence a rib, with cordial spirits warm,
And life-blood streaming fresh; wide was the
    wound,
But suddenly with flesh filled up and healed:
The rib he formed and fashioned with his
    hands;
Under his forming hands a creature grew,
Manlike, but different sex, so lovely fair,
That what seemed fair in all the world seemed
    now
Mean, or in her summed up, in her contained,
And in her looks, which from that time infused
Sweetness into my heart, unfelt before,
And into all things from her air inspired
The spirit of love and amorous delight.

She disappeared, and left me dark; I waked
To find her, or forever to deplore
Her loss, and other pleasures all abjure:
When out of hope, behold her, not far off,
Such as I saw her in my dream, adorned
With what all earth or Heaven could bestow
To make her amiable. On she came,
Led by her heavenly Maker, though unseen,
And guided by his voice, nor uninformed
Of nuptial sanctity and marriage rites:
Grace was in all her steps, Heaven in her eye,
In every gesture dignity and love.
I, overjoyed, could not forbear aloud:
    "This turn hath made amends; thou hast
        fulfilled
Thy words, Creator bounteous and benign,
Giver of all things fair, but fairest this
Of all thy gifts, nor enviest. I now see
Bone of my bone, flesh of my flesh, myself
Before me; Woman is her name, of man
Extracted: for this cause he shall forego
Father and mother, and to his wife adhere;
And they shall be one flesh, one heart, one
        soul."
    She heard me thus, and though divinely
        brought,
Yet innocence and virgin modesty,
Her virtue and the conscience of her worth,
That would be wooed, and not unsought be
    won,

Not obvious, not obtrusive, but retired,
The more desirable; or, to say all,
Nature herself, though pure of sinful thought,
Wrought in her so, that, seeing me, she turned;
I followed her; she what was honor knew,
And with obsequious majesty approved
My pleaded reason. To the nuptial bower
I led her blushing like the morn: all Heaven,
And happy constellations on that hour
Shed their selectest influence; the earth
Gave sign of gratulation, and each hill;
Joyous the birds; fresh gales and gentle airs
Whispered it to the woods, and from their
     wings
Flung rose, flung odors from the spicy shrub,
Disporting, till the amorous bird of night
Sung spousal, and bid haste the evening star
On his hill-top, to light the bridal lamp.

. . .

               When I approach
Her loveliness, so absolute she seems,
And in herself complete, so well to know
Her own, that what she wills to do or say
Seems wisest, virtuousest, discreetest, best;
All higher knowledge in her presence falls
Degraded, wisdom in discourse with her
Loses discountenanced, and like folly shows;
Authority and reason on her wait,
As one intended first, not after made

Occasionally; and, to consummate all,
Greatness of mind and nobleness their seat
Build in her loveliest, and create an awe
About her, as a guard angelic placed,

. . .

Neither her outside formed so fair, nor aught

. . .

So much delights me, as those graceful acts,
Those thousand decencies that daily flow
From all her words and actions, mixed with
        love
And sweet compliance, which declare unfeigned
Union of mind, or in us both one soul;
Harmony to behold in wedded pair
More grateful than harmonious sound to the
        ear.

A Bridal Song

William Shakespeare
1564–1616

Roses, their sharp spines being gone,
Not royal in their smells alone,
But in their hue;
Maiden pinks, of odour faint,
Daisies smell-less, yet most quaint,
And sweet thyme true;

Primrose, firstborn child of Ver,
Merry springtime's harbinger,
With her bells dim;
Oxlips in their cradles growing,
Marigolds on death-beds blowing,
Larks'-heels trim:

All dear Nature's children sweet
Lie 'fore bride and bridegroom's feet,
Blessing their sense.
Not an angel of the air,
Bird melodious or bird fair,
Be absent hence.

The crow, the slanderous cuckoo, nor
The boding raven, nor chough hoar,
   Nor chattering pie,
May on our bride-house perch or sing,
Or with them any discord bring,
   But from it fly.

'Twas When the Spousal Time of May

COVENTRY PATMORE
1823–1896

'Twas when the spousal time of May
    Hangs all the hedge with bridal wreaths,
And air's so sweet the bosom gay
    Gives thanks for every breath it breathes;
When like to like is gladly moved,
    And each thing joins in Spring's refrain,
'Let those love now who never loved;
    'Let those who have loved love again;'
That I, in whom the sweet time wrought,
    Lay stretch'd within a lonely glade,
Abandon'd to delicious thought,
    Beneath the softly twinkling shade.
The leaves, all stirring, mimick'd well
    A neighbouring rush of rivers cold,
And, as the sun or shadow fell,
    So these were green and those were gold;
In dim recesses hyacinths droop'd,
    And breadths of primrose lit the air,
Which, wandering through the woodland,
      stoop'd
    And gather'd perfumes here and there;

Upon the spray the squirrel swung,
    And careless songsters, six or seven,
Sang lofty songs the leaves among,
    Fit for their only listener, Heaven.

Bridal Song

THOMAS LOVELL BEDDOES
1803–1849

By female voices
We have bathed, where none have seen us,
In the lake and in the fountain,
Underneath the charmed statue
Of the timid, bending Venus,
When the water-nymphs were counting
In the waves the stars of night,
And those maidens started at you,
Your limbs shone through so soft and bright.
But no secrets dare we tell,
For thy slaves unlace thee,
And he who shall embrace thee,
Waits to try thy beauty's spell.

By male voices

We have crowned thee queen of women,
 Since love's love, the rose, hath kept her
  Court within thy lips and blushes,
And thine eye, in beauty swimming,
 Kissing, rendered up the sceptre,
At whose touch the startled soul
 Like an ocean bounds and gushes,
And spirits bend at thy controul.
  But no secrets dare we tell,
   For thy slaves unlace thee,
   And he, who shall embrace thee,
  Is at hand, and so farewell.

Bridal Song

GEORGE CHAPMAN
1559–1634

O! come, soft rest of cares, come Night,
　　Come, naked Virtue's only tire,
The reapèd harvest of the light,
　　Bound up in sheaves of sacred fire.
　　　　Love calls to war;
　　　　　Sighs his alarms,
　　　　　Lips his swords are
　　　　　The field his arms.

Come, Night, and lay thy velvet hand
　　On glorious Day's outfacing face;
And all thy crownèd flames command,
　　For torches to our nuptial grace.
　　　　Love calls to war;
　　　　　Sighs his alarms,
　　　　　Lips his swords are
　　　　　The field his arms.

Minstrels' Marriage-Song *from* "Ælla: A Tragical Interlude"

Thomas Chatterton

1752–1770

First Minstrel

The budding floweret blushes at the light:
  The meads are sprinkled with the yellow
    hue;
In daisied mantles is the mountain dight;
  The slim young cowslip bendeth with the
    dew;
The trees enleafèd, into heaven straught,
When gentle winds do blow, to whistling din
  are brought.

The evening comes and brings the dew along;
  The ruddy welkin sheeneth to the eyne;
Around the ale-stake minstrels sing the song;
  Young ivy round the doorpost doth entwine;
I lay me on the grass; yet, to my will,
Albeit all is fair, there lacketh something still.

Second Minstrel

So Adam thought, what time, in Paradise,
    All heaven and earth did homage to his
      mind.
In woman and none else man's pleasaunce lies,
    As instruments of joy are kind with kind.
Go, take a wife unto thine arms, and see
Winter and dusky hills will have a charm for
    thee.

Esthonian Bridal Song

JOHANN GOTTFRIED VON HERDER
1744–1803

Deck thyself, maiden,
With the hood of thy mother;
Put on the ribands
Which thy mother once wore:
On thy head the band of duty,
On thy forehead the band of care.
Sit in the seat of thy mother,
And walk in thy mother's footsteps.
And weep not, weep not, maiden:
If thou weepest in thy bridal attire,
Thou wilt weep all thy life.

TRANSLATED BY W. TAYLOR

On the Marriage of T.K. and C.C.: The Morning Stormy

THOMAS CAREW
c. 1595–c. 1639

Such should this day be, so the sun should hide
His bashful face, and let the conquering Bride
Without a rival shine, whilst he forbears
To mingle his unequal beams with hers;
Or if sometimes he glance his squinting eye
Between the parting clouds, 'tis but to spy,
Not emulate her glories, so comes dressed
In veils, but as a masquer to the feast.
Thus heaven should lower, such stormy gusts
    should blow
Not to denounce ungentle Fates, but show
The cheerful Bridegroom to the clouds and
    wind
Hath all his tears, and all his sighs assigned.
Let tempests struggle in the air, but rest
Eternal calms within thy peaceful breast,
Thrice happy Youth; but ever sacrifice
To that fair hand that dried thy blubbered eyes,
That crowned thy head with roses, and turned
    all
The plagues of love into a cordial,

When first it joined her virgin snow to thine,
Which when today the Priest shall recombine,
From the mysterious holy touch such charms
Will flow, as shall unlock her wreathèd arms,
And open a free passage to that fruit
Which thou hast toiled for with a long pursuit.
But ere thou feed, that thou may'st better taste
Thy present joys, think on thy torments past.
Think on the mercy freed thee, think upon
Her virtues, graces, beauties, one by one,
So shalt thou relish all, enjoy the whole
Delights of her fair body, and pure soul.
Then boldly to the fight of love proceed,
'Tis mercy not to pity though she bleed,
We'll strew no nuts, but change that ancient
    form,
For till tomorrow we'll prorogue this storm,
Which shall confound with its loud whistling
    noise
Her pleasing shrieks, and fan thy panting joys.

The Poet's Bridal-Day Song

ALLAN CUNNINGHAM
1784–1842

O, my love's like the steadfast sun,
Or streams that deepen as they run;
Nor hoary hairs, nor forty years,
Nor moments between sighs and tears,
Nor nights of thought, nor days of pain,
Nor dreams of glory dreamed in vain,
Nor mirth, nor sweetest song that flows
To sober joys and soften woes,
Can make my heart or fancy flee,
One moment, my sweet wife, from thee.

Even while I muse, I see thee sit
In maiden bloom and matron wit;
Fair, gentle as when first I sued,
Ye seem, but of sedater mood;
Yet my heart leaps as fond for thee
As when, beneath Arbigland tree,
We stayed and wooed, and thought the moon
Set on the sea an hour too soon;
Or lingered mid the falling dew,
When looks were fond and words were few.

Though I see smiling at thy feet
Five sons and ae fair daughter sweet,
And time, and care, and birthtime woes
Have dimmed thine eye and touched thy rose,
To thee, and thoughts of thee, belong
Whate'er charms me in tale or song.
When words descend like dews, unsought,
With gleams of deep, enthusiast thought,
And Fancy in her heaven flies free,
They come, my love, they come from thee.

O, when more thought we gave, of old,
To silver than some give to gold,
'T was sweet to sit and ponder o'er
How we should deck our humble bower;
'T was sweet to pull, in hope, with thee,
The golden fruit of fortune's tree;
And sweeter still to choose and twine
A garland for that brow of thine,—
A song-wreath which may grace my Jean,
While rivers flow, and woods grow green.

At times there come, as come there ought,
Grave moments of sedater thought,
When Fortune frowns, nor lends our night
One gleam of her inconstant light;
And Hope, that decks the peasant's bower,
Shines like a rainbow through the shower;
O, then I see, while seated nigh,
A mother's heart shine in thine eye,
And proud resolve and purpose meek,
Speak of thee more than words can speak.
I think this wedded wife of mine
The best of all that's not divine.

Like a Laverock in the Lift

JEAN INGELOW
1820–1897

It's we two, it's we two for aye,
All the world, and we two, and Heaven be our
    stay!
Like a laverock in the lift, sing, O bonny bride!
All the world was Adam once, with Eve by his
        side.
What's the world, my lass, my love!—what can
        it do?
I am thine, and thou art mine; life is sweet and
        new.
If the world have missed the mark, let it stand
        by;
For we two have gotten leave, and once more
        will try.

Like a laverock in the lift, sing, O bonny bride!
It's we two, it's we two, happy side by side.
Take a kiss from me, thy man; now the song
        begins:
"All is made afresh for us, and the brave heart
        wins."

When the darker days come, and no sun will
    shine,
Thou shalt dry my tears, lass, and I'll dry
    thine.
It's we two, it's we two, while the world's away,
Sitting by the golden sheaves on our wedding
    day.

laverock = lark, lift = cloud

Marriage Morning

ALFRED, LORD TENNYSON
1809–1892

Light, so low upon earth,
    You send a flash to the sun.
Here is the golden close of love,
    All my wooing is done.
Oh, the woods and the meadows,
    Woods where we hid from the wet,
Stiles where we stay'd to be kind,
    Meadows in which we met!

Light, so low in the vale
    You flash and lighten afar,
For this is the golden morning of love,
    And you are his morning star.
Flash, I am coming, I come,
    By meadow and stile and wood,
Oh, lighten into my eyes and heart,
    Into my heart and my blood!

Heart, are you great enough
  For a love that never tires?
O heart, are you great enough for love?
  I have heard of thorns and briers.
Over the thorns and briers,
  Over the meadows and stiles,
Over the world to the end of it
  Flash for a million miles.

From "The Bells"

EDGAR ALLAN POE
1809–1849

Hear the mellow wedding bells
Golden bells!
What a world of happiness their harmony foretells!
Through the balmy air of night
How they ring out their delight!—
From the molten-golden notes,
And all in tune,
What a liquid ditty floats
To the turtle-dove that listens, while she gloats
On the moon!
Oh, from out the sounding cells,
What a gush of euphony voluminously wells!
How it swells!
How it dwells
On the Future!—how it tells
Of the rapture that impels
To the swinging and the ringing
Of the bells, bells, bells—
Of the bells, bells, bells, bells,
Bells, bells, bells—
To the rhyming and the chiming of the bells!

Between Us a New Morning

PAUL ELUARD
1895–1952

Between us a new morning
Is being born from our flesh
Just the right way
To put everything into shape
We are moving just the right footsteps ahead
And the earth says hello to us
The day has all our rainbows
The fireplace is lit with our eyes
And the ocean celebrates our marriage

TRANSLATED BY WALTER LOWENFELS

Not from Pride, but from Humility

JAMES LAWSON
1938–

Not from pride, but from humility
As mortals, with human weaknesses
And strengths
You stand alone today
And promise faith.
Your faith you find as you live,
Each moment consecrated to
A search for Truth
And for that Good
Whose presence you have deeply felt.

NOW:
From this time, until
The time you must rejoin the
Earth from which you came,
Love the love in you that underlies
Your actions.
And with each other,
Share your wonder at the beauty
That you find
As Man and Wife.

From A Slave Marriage Ceremony

Dark an' stormy may come de wedder;
I jines dis he-male an' dis she-male togedder.
Let none, but Him dat makes de thunder,
Put dis he-male an' dis she-male asunder.
I darfore 'nounce you bofe de same.
Be good, go 'long, an' keep up yo' name.
De broomstick's jumped, de worl's not wide.
She's now yo' own. Salute yo' bride!

Navajo Chant

Rising Sun! when you shall shine,
  Make this house happy,

Beautify it with your beams;
  Make this house happy,

God of Dawn! your white blessings spread;
  Make this house happy.

Guard the doorway from all evil;
  Make this house happy.

White corn! Abide herein;
  Make this house happy.

Soft wealth! May this hut cover much;
  Make this house happy.

Heavy Rain! Your virtues send;
  Make this house happy.

Corn Pollen! Bestow content;
  Make this house happy.

May peace around this family dwell;
  Make this house happy.

Marriage

Samuel Rogers
1763–1855

Then before all they stand—the holy vow
And ring of gold, no fond illusions now,
Bind her as his. Across the threshold led,
And every tear kissed off as soon as shed,
His house she enters—there to be a light,
Shining within, when all without is night;
A guardian angel o'er his life presiding,
Doubling his pleasures and his cares dividing,
Winning him back when mingling in the
    throng,
Back from a world we love, alas! too long,
To fireside happiness, to hours of ease,
Blest with that charm, the certainty to please.
How oft her eyes read his; her gentle mind
To all his wishes, all his thoughts inclined;
Still subject—ever on the watch to borrow
Mirth of his mirth and sorrow of his sorrow!
The soul of music slumbers in the shell,
Till waked and kindled by the master's spell,
And feeling hearts—touch them but rightly—
    pour
A thousand melodies unheard before!

The Newly-Wedded

Winthrop Mackworth Praed
1802–1839

Now the rite is duly done,
　Now the word is spoken,
And the spell has made us one
　Which may ne'er be broken;
Rest we, dearest, in our home,
　Roam we o'er the heather:
We shall rest, and we shall roam,
　Shall we not? together.

From this hour the summer rose
　Sweeter breathes to charm us;
From this hour the winter snows
　Lighter fall to harm us:
Fair or foul—on land or sea—
　Come the wind or weather,
Best and worst whate'er they be,
　We shall share together.

Death, who friend from friend can part,
　Brother rend from brother,
Shall but link us, heart and heart,
　Closer to each other:

We will call his anger play,
  Deem his dart a feather,
When we meet him on our way
  Hand in hand together.

Nuptial Sleep

DANTE GABRIEL ROSSETTI
1828–1882

At length their long kiss severed, with sweet
smart:
And as the last slow sudden drops are shed
From sparkling eaves when all the storm has
fled,
So singly flagged the pulses of each heart.
Their bosoms sundered, with the opening start
Of married flowers to either side outspread
From the knit stem; yet still their mouths,
burnt red,
Fawned on each other where they lay apart.

Sleep sank them lower than the tide of dreams,
And their dreams watched them sink, and
slid away.
Slowly their souls swam up again, through
gleams
Of watered light and dull drowned waifs of
day;
Till from some wonder of new woods and
streams
He woke, and wondered more: for there she
lay.

Nuptial Song

"Sigh, Heart, Break Not"

John Leicester Warren,
Lord de Tabley
1835–1895

Sigh, heart, and break not; rest, lark, and wake
    not!
    Day I hear coming to draw my Love away.
As mere-waves whisper, and clouds grow
    crisper,
    Ah, like a rose he will waken up with day.

In moon-light lonely, he is my Love only,
    I share with none when Luna rides in grey.
As dawn-beams quicken, my rivals thicken,
    The light and deed and turmoil of the day.

To watch my sleeper to me is sweeter,
    Than any waking words my Love can say;
In dream he finds me and closer winds me!
    Let him rest by me a little more and stay.

Ah, mine eyes, close not: and, tho' he knows
    not,
    My lips, on his be tender while you may;
Ere leaves are shaken, and ring-doves waken,
    And infant buds begin to scent new day.

Fair Darkness, measure thine hours, as treasure
    Shed each one slowly from thine urn, I pray;
Hoard in and cover each from my lover;
    I cannot lose him yet; dear night, delay.

Each moment dearer, true-love, lie nearer,
    My hair shall blind thee lest thou see the
        ray;
My locks encumber thine ears in slumber,
    Lest any bird dare give thee note of day.

He rests so calmly; we lie so warmly;
    Hand within hand, as children after play;—
In shafted amber on roof and chamber
    Dawn enters; my Love wakens; here is day.

Love's Philosophy

PERCY BYSSHE SHELLEY
1792–1822

The fountains mingle with the river
    And the rivers with the Ocean,
The winds of Heaven mix for ever
    With a sweet emotion;
Nothing in the world is single;
    All things by a law divine
In one spirit meet and mingle.
    Why not I with thine?—

See the mountains kiss high Heaven
    And the waves clasp one another;
No sister-flower would be forgiven
    If it disdained its brother;
And the sunlight clasps the earth
    And the moonbeams kiss the sea:
What is all this sweet work worth
    If thou kiss not me?

Love

GEORGE GORDON, LORD BYRON
1788–1824

Yes, love indeed is light from heaven;
    A spark of that immortal fire
With angels shared, by Alla given,
    To lift from earth our low desire.
Devotion wafts the mind above,
But heaven itself descends in love;
A feeling from the Godhead caught,
To wean from self each sordid thought;
A ray of Him who formed the whole;
A glory circling round the soul!

What Thing Is Love?

GEORGE PEELE

1556–1596

What thing is love? for sure love is a thing.
It is a prick, it is a sting,
It is a pretty, pretty thing;
It is a fire, it is a coal,
Whose flame creeps in at every hole;
And as my wit doth best devise,
Love's dwelling is in ladies' eyes,
From whence do glance love's piercing darts,
That make such holes into our hearts;
And all the world herein accord,
Love is a great and mighty lord;
And when he list to mount so high,
With Venus he in heaven doth lie,
And evermore hath been a god,
Since Mars and she played even and odd.

I Will Tell Thee What It Is to Love

CHARLES SWAIN
1803–1874

Love? I will tell thee what it is to love!
It is to build with human thoughts a shrine,
Where Hope sits brooding like a beauteous
    dove;
Where Time seems young, and Life a thing
    divine.
All tastes, all pleasures, all desires combine
To consecrate this sanctuary of bliss.
Above, the stars in cloudless beauty shine;
Around, the streams their flowery margins kiss;
And if there's heaven on earth, that heaven is
    surely this.

Yes, this is love, the steadfast and the true,
The immortal glory which hath never set;
The best, the brightest boon the heart e'er
    knew:
Of all life's sweets the very sweetest yet!
O' who but can recall the eve they met
To breathe, in some green walk, their first
    young vow?

While summer flowers with moonlight dews
    were wet,
And winds sighed soft around the mountain's
    brow,
And all was rapture then which is but memory
    now!

So Well I Love Thee

MICHAEL DRAYTON
1563–1631

So well I love thee, as without thee I
Love nothing; if I might choose, I'd rather die
Than be one day debarr'd thy company.

Since beasts, and plants do grow, and live and
   move,
Beasts are those men, that such a life approve:
He only lives, that deadly is in love.

The corn that in the ground is sown first dies
And of one seed do many ears arise:
Love, this world's corn, by dying multiplies.

The seeds of love first by thy eyes were thrown
Into a ground untill'd, a heart unknown
To bear such fruit, till by thy hands 'twas sown.

Look as your looking-glass by chance may fall,
Divide and break in many pieces small
And yet shows forth the selfsame face in all:

Proportions, features, graces just the same,
And in the smallest piece as well the name
Of fairest one deserves, as in the richest frame.

So all my thoughts are pieces but of you
Which put together makes a glass so true
As I therein no other's face but yours can view.

He Will Praise His Lady

GUIDO GUINIZELLI
1230?–1276?

Yea, let me praise my lady whom I love:
    Likening her unto the lily and rose:
    Brighter than morning star her visage glows;
She is beneath even as her Saint above;
She is as the air in summer which God wove
    Of purple and of vermilion glorious;
    As gold and jewels richer than man knows.
Love's self, being love for her, must holier
        prove.
Ever as she walks she hath a sober grace,
    Making bold men abashed and good men
        glad;
        If she delight thee not, thy heart must
        err.
No man dare look on her, his thoughts being
        base:
    Nay, let me say even more than I have
        said;—
        No man could think base thoughts who
        looked on her.

TRANSLATED BY DANTE GABRIEL ROSSETTI

My Lady

DANTE ALIGHIERI
1265–1321

So gentle and so gracious doth appear
    My lady when she giveth her salute,
    That every tongue becometh trembling,
        mute;
Nor do the eyes to look upon her dare.
Although she hears her praises, she doth go
    Benignly vested with humility;
    And like a thing come down she seems to be
From heaven to earth, a miracle to show.
So pleaseth she whoever cometh nigh,
    She gives the heart a sweetness through the
        eyes,
    Which none can understand who doth not
        prove.
And from her countenance there seems to move
    A spirit sweet and in Love's very guise,
    Who to the soul, in going, sayeth: Sigh!

TRANSLATED BY CHARLES ELIOT NORTON

She Walks in Beauty

George Gordon, Lord Byron
1788–1824

1

She walks in beauty, like the night
    Of cloudless climes and starry skies;
And all that's best of dark and bright
    Meet in her aspect and her eyes:
Thus mellowed to that tender light
    Which heaven to gaudy day denies.

2

One shade the more, one ray the less,
    Had half impaired the nameless grace
Which waves in every raven tress,
    Or softly lightens o'er her face;
Where thoughts serenely sweet express
    How pure, how dear their dwelling place.

3

And on that cheek, and o'er that brow,
    So soft, so calm, yet eloquent,
The smiles that win, the tints that glow,
    But tell of days in goodness spent,
A mind at peace with all below,
    A heart whose love is innocent!

When Our Two Souls
Stand Up Erect and Strong

ELIZABETH BARRETT BROWNING
1806–1861

When our two souls stand up erect and strong,
Face to face, silent, drawing nigh and nigher,
Until the lengthening wings break into fire
At either curvèd point—what bitter wrong
Can the earth do to us, that we should not long
Be here contented? Think. In mounting higher,
The angels would press on us and aspire
To drop some golden orb of perfect song
Into our deep, dear silence. Let us stay
Rather on earth, beloved—where the unfit
Contrarious moods of men recoil away
And isolate pure spirits, and permit
A place to stand and love in for a day,
With darkness and the death-hour rounding it.

So Are You to My Thoughts as Food to Life

WILLIAM SHAKESPEARE
1564–1616

So are you to my thoughts as food to life,
Or as sweet-season'd showers are to the ground;
And for the peace of you I hold such strife
As 'twixt a miser and his wealth is found;
Now proud as an enjoyer, and anon
Doubting the filching age will steal his treasure;
Now counting best to be with you alone,
Then better'd that the world may see my
    pleasure:
Sometime all full with feasting on your sight,
And by and by clean starved for a look;
Possessing or pursuing no delight,
Save what is had or must from you be took.
      Thus do I pine and surfeit day by day,
      Or gluttoning on all, or all away.

Your Hands Lie Open in the Long Fresh Grass

DANTE GABRIEL ROSSETTI
1828–1882

Your hands lie open in the long fresh grass,
The finger-points look through like rosy
   blooms;
Your eyes smile peace. The pasture gleams and
   glooms
'Neath billowing skies that scatter and amass.
All round our nest, far as the eye can pass,
Are golden kingcup-fields with silver edge
Where the cow-parsley skirts the hawthorn-
   hedge.
'Tis visible silence, still as the hourglass.
Deep in the sun-searched growths the dragonfly
Hangs like a blue thread loosened from the sky.
So this winged hour is dropt to us from above.
Oh! clasp we to our hearts, for deathless dower,
This close-companioned inarticulate hour
When twofold silence was the song of love.

One Day I Wrote Her Name Upon the Strand

EDMUND SPENSER
1552?–1599

One day I wrote her name upon the strand,
  But came the waves and washèd it away:
Again I wrote it with a second hand,
  But came the tide, and made my pains his
    prey.
'Vain man,' said she, 'thou do'st in vain assay,
  A mortal thing so to immortalize,
For I myself shall like to this decay,
  And eek my name be wipèd out likewise.'
'Not so,' quoth I, 'let baser things devise
  To die in dust, but you shall live by fame:
My verse your virtues rare shall eternize,
  And in the heavens write your glorious
    name,
    Where, whenas death shall all the world
      subdue,
    Our love shall live, and later life renew.'

Shall I Compare Thee to a Summer's Day?

WILLIAM SHAKESPEARE
1564–1616

Shall I compare thee to a summer's day?
   Thou art more lovely and more temperate:
Rough winds do shake the darling buds of May,
   And summer's lease hath all too short a date:
Sometime too hot the eye of heaven shines,
   And often is his gold complexion dimmed;
And every fair from fair sometime declines,
   By chance, or nature's changing course
      untrimmed;
But thy eternal summer shall not fade,
   Nor lose possession of that fair thou owest,
Nor shall death brag thou wanderest in his
   shade,
   When in eternal lines to time thou growest;
     So long as men can breathe, or eyes can
see,
     So long lives this, and this gives life to
thee.

Let Me Not to the Marriage of True Minds

WILLIAM SHAKESPEARE
1564–1616

Let me not to the marriage of true minds
Admit impediments: love is not love,
Which alters when it alteration finds,
Or bends with the remover to remove;
O, no! it is an ever-fixèd mark,
That looks on tempests, and is never shaken;
It is the star to every wandering bark,
Whose worth's unknown, although his height
    be taken.
Love's not Time's fool, though rosy lips and
    cheeks
Within his bending sickle's compass come;
Love alters not with his brief hours and weeks,
But bears it out even to the edge of doom.
   If this be error, and upon me proved,
   I never writ, nor no man ever loved.

If I Leave All for Thee

ELIZABETH BARRETT BROWNING
1806–1861

If I leave all for thee, wilt thou exchange
And be all to me? Shall I never miss
Home-talk and blessing and the common kiss
That comes to each in turn, nor count it
    strange,
When I look up, to drop on a new range
Of walls and floors, another home than this?
Nay, wilt thou fill that place by me which is
Filled by dead eyes too tender to know change
That's hardest? If to conquer love, has tried,
To conquer grief, tries more, as all things prove,
For grief indeed is love and grief beside.
Alas, I have grieved so I am hard to love.
Yet love me—wilt thou? Open thine heart
    wide,
And fold within the wet wings of thy dove.

Love in a Life

ROBERT BROWNING
1812–1889

Room after room,
I hunt the house through
We inhabit together.
Heart, fear nothing, for, heart, thou shalt find
    her—
Next time, herself!—not the trouble behind her
Left in the curtain, the couch's perfume!
As she brushed it, the cornice-wreath blossomed
    anew:
Yon looking-glass gleamed at the wave of her
    feather.

Yet the day wears,
And door succeeds door;
I try the fresh fortune—
Range the wide house from the wing to the
    centre.
Still the same chance! she goes out as I enter.
Spend my whole day in the quest,—who cares?
But 'tis twilight, you see,—with such suites to
    explore,
Such closets to search, such alcoves to
    importune!

Surrender

EMILY DICKINSON
1830–1886

Doubt me, my dim companion!
Why, God would be content
With but a fraction of the love
Poured thee without a stint.
The whole of me, forever,
What more the woman can—
Say quick, that I may dower thee
With last delight I own!

It cannot be my spirit,
For that was thine before;
I ceded all of dust I knew—
What opulence the more
Had I, a humble maiden,
Whose farthest of degree
Was that she might,
Some distant heaven,
Dwell timidly with thee!

Kissing Her Hair

ALGERNON CHARLES SWINBURNE
1837–1909

Kissing her hair, I sat against her feet:
Wove and unwove it,—wound, and found it
    sweet;
Made fast therewith her hands, drew down her
    eyes,
Deep as deep flowers, and dreamy like dim
    skies;
With her own tresses bound, and found her
    fair,—
      Kissing her hair.

Sleep were no sweeter than her face to me,—
Sleep of cold sea-bloom under the cold sea:
What pain could get between my face and
    hers?
What new sweet thing would Love not relish
    worse?
Unless, perhaps, white Death had kissed me
    there,—
      Kissing her hair.

The Ecstasy

JOHN DONNE
1572–1631

Where, like a pillow on a bed,
    A pregnant bank swelled up, to rest
The violet's reclining head,
    Sat we two, one another's best.

Our hands were firmly cemented
    With a fast balm, which thence did spring;
Our eye-beams twisted, and did thread
    Our eyes upon one double string;

So to entergraft our hands, as yet
    Was all our means to make us one,
And pictures on our eyes to get
    Was all our propagation.

As 'twixt two equal armies Fate
    Suspends uncertain victory,
Our souls (which to advance their state
    Were gone out) hung 'twixt her and me.

And whilst our souls negotiate there,
    We like sepulchral statues lay;
All day the same our postures were,
    And we said nothing all the day.

If any, so by love refined
    That he soul's language understood,
And by good love were grown all mind,
    Within convenient distance stood,

He (though he knew not which soul spake,
    Because both meant, both spake the same)
Might thence a new concoction take,
    And part far purer than he came.

This ecstasy doth unperplex
    (We said) and tell us what we love,
We see by this, it was not sex,
    We see, we saw not what did move:

But as all several souls contain
    Mixture of things, they know not what,
Love these mixed souls doth mix again,
    And makes both one, each this and that.

A single violet transplant,
    The strength, the colour, and the size,
(All which before was poor and scant)
    Redoubles still, and multiplies.

When love with one another so
    Interinanimates two souls,
That abler soul, which thence doth flow,
    Defects of loneliness controls.

We then, who are this new soul, know
    Of what we are composed, and made,
For the atomies of which we grow
    Are souls, whom no change can invade.

But, O alas! so long, so far
    Our bodies why do we forbear?
They are ours, though they are not we; we are
    The intelligences, they the sphere.

We owe them thanks, because they thus
    Did us, to us, at first convey,
Yielded their forces, sense, to us,
    Nor are dross to us, but allay.

On man heaven's influence works not so,
    But that it first imprints the air;
So soul into the soul may flow,
    Though it to body first repair.

As our blood labours to beget
    Spirits, as like souls as it can;
Because such fingers need to knit
    That subtle knot, which makes us man;

So must pure lovers' souls descend
    To affections, and to faculties,
Which sense may reach and apprehend,
    Else a great Prince in prison lies.

To our bodies turn we then, that so
    Weak men on love revealed may look;
Love's mysteries in souls do grow,
    But yet the body is his book.

And if some lover, such as we,
    Have heard this dialogue of one,
Let him still mark us, he shall see
    Small change, when we're to bodies gone.

From Paterson

WILLIAM CARLOS WILLIAMS
1883–1963

Your lovely hands
Your lovely tender hands!
Reflections of what grace
what heavenly joy

predicted for the world
in knowing you—
blest, as am I, and humbled
by such ecstasy.

She Tells Her Love While Half Asleep

ROBERT GRAVES
1895–1985

She tells her love while half asleep
   In the dark hours,
      With half-words whispered low:
As Earth stirs in her winter sleep
   And puts out grass and flowers
      Despite the snow,
      Despite the falling snow.

Daybreak

STEPHEN SPENDER
1909–

At dawn she lay with her profile at that angle
Which, sleeping, seems the stone face of an
 angel;
Her hair a harp the hand of a breeze follows
To play, against the white cloud of the pillows.
Then in flush of rose she woke, and her eyes
 were open
Swimming with blue through the rose of dawn.
From her dew of lips, the drop of one word
Fell, from a dawn of fountains, when she
 murmured
"Darling" upon my heart the song of the first
 bird.
"My dream glides in my dream," she said,
 "come true.
I waken from you to my dream of you."
O then my waking dream dared assume
The audacity of her sleep. Our dreams
Flowed into each other's arms, like dreams.

Gloire de Dijon

D. H. LAWRENCE
1885–1930

When she rises in the morning
I linger to watch her;
She spreads the bath-cloth underneath the
    window
And the sunbeams catch her
Glistening white on the shoulders,
While down her sides the mellow
Golden shadow glows as
She stoops to the sponge, and her swung breasts
Sway like full-blown yellow
Gloire de Dijon roses.

She drips herself with water, and her shoulders
Glisten as silver, they crumple up
Like wet and falling roses, and I listen
For the sluicing of their rain-dishevelled petals.
In the window full of sunlight
Concentrates her golden shadow
Fold on fold, until it glows as
Mellow as the glory roses.

The Good-Morrow

JOHN DONNE
1572–1631

I wonder, by my troth, what thou and I
Did, till we loved? were we not weaned till
  then?
But sucked on country pleasures, childishly?
Or snorted we in the Seven Sleepers' den?
'Twas so; but this, all pleasures fancies be.
If ever any beauty I did see,
Which I desired, and got, 'twas but a dream of
  thee.

And now good-morrow to our waking souls,
Which watch not one another out of fear;
For love, all love of other sights controls,
And makes one little room an everywhere.
Let sea-discoverers to new worlds have gone,
Let maps to others, worlds on worlds have
  shown,
Let us possess one world, each hath one, and is
  one.

My face in thine eye, thine in mine appears,
And true plain hearts do in the faces rest;
Where can we find two better hemispheres,
Without sharp north, without declining west?
Whatever dies was not mixed equally;
If our two loves be one, or, thou and I
Love so alike that none do slacken, none can
   die.

The Ragged Wood

WILLIAM BUTLER YEATS
1865–1939

O hurry where by water among the trees
The delicate-stepping stag and his lady sigh,
When they have but looked upon their
    images—
Would none had ever loved but you and I!

Or have you heard that sliding silver-shoed
Pale silver-proud queen-woman of the sky,
When the sun looked out of his golden
    hood?—
O that none ever loved but you and I!

O hurry to the ragged wood, for there
I will drive all those lovers out and cry—
O my share of the world, O yellow hair!
No one has ever loved but you and I.

The Sun Rising

JOHN DONNE
1572–1631

Busy old fool, unruly Sun,
      Why dost thou thus,
Through windows, and through curtains call on
    us?
Must to thy motions lovers' seasons run?
      Saucy pedantic wretch, go chide
      Late school-boys, and sour 'prentices,
    Go tell court-huntsmen that the King will
    ride,
    Call country ants to harvest offices;
Love, all alike, no season knows, nor clime,
Nor hours, days, months, which are the rags of
    time.

      Thy beams, so reverend, and strong
      Why shouldst thou think?
I could eclipse and cloud them with a wink,
But that I would not lose her sight so long:
      If her eyes have not blinded thine,
      Look, and tomorrow late, tell me,
    Whether both the Indias of spice and
      mine
    Be where thou left'st them, or lie here
      with me.

Ask for those kings whom thou saw'st yesterday,
And thou shalt hear, 'All here in one bed lay.'

She is all States, and all Princes, I;
Nothing else is.
Princes do but play us; compar'd to this,
All honour's mimic; all wealth alchemy.
Thou Sun art half as happy as we,
In that the world's contracted thus;
Thine age asks ease, and since thy duties
be
To warm the world, that's done in warming
us.
Shine here to us, and thou art every where;
This bed thy centre is, these walls, thy sphere.

Only We

RICHARD MONCKTON MILNES,
LORD HOUGHTON
1809–1885

Dream no more that grief and pain
Could such hearts as ours enchain,
Safe from loss and safe from gain,
　　Free, as love makes free.

When false friends pass coldly by,
Sigh, in earnest pity, sigh,
Turning thine unclouded eye
　　Up from them to me.

Hear not danger's trampling feet,
Feel not sorrow's wintry sleet,
Trust that life is just and meet,
　　With mine arm round thee.

Lip on lip, and eye to eye,
Love to love, we live, we die;
No more thou, and no more I,
　　We, and only we!

Most Like an Arch This Marriage

JOHN CIARDI
1916–1985

Most like an arch—an entrance which upholds
and shores the stone-crush up the air like lace.
Mass made idea, and idea held in place.
A lock in time. Inside half-heaven unfolds.

Most like an arch—two weaknesses that lean
into a strength. Two fallings become firm.
Two joined abeyances become a term
naming the fact that teaches fact to mean.

Not quite that? Not much less. World as it is,
what's strong and separate falters. All I do
at piling stone on stone apart from you
is roofless around nothing. Till we kiss

I am no more than upright and unset.
It is by falling in and in we make
the all-bearing point, for one another's sake,
in faultless failing, raised by our own weight.

On Marriage

HIPPONAX
c. 540 B.C.

Marriage is best for any prudent man;
No better gift than woman's aid is found.
Her very marriage-portion often can
Save house and home; and when she is around,
He has a helper, not a mistress, who
With her good sense stands firm his whole life
    through.

Love Song: I and Thou

ALAN DUGAN
1923–

Nothing is plumb, level, or square:
　　the studs are bowed, the joists
are shaky by nature, no piece fits
　　any other piece without a gap
or pinch, and bent nails
　　dance all over the surfacing
like maggots. By Christ
　　I am no carpenter. I built
the roof for myself, the walls
　　for myself, the floors
for myself, and got
　　hung up in it myself. I
danced with a purple thumb
　　at this house-warming, drunk
with my prime whiskey: rage.
　　Oh I spat rage's nails
into the frame-up of my work:
　　it held. It settled plumb,
level, solid, square and true
　　for that great moment. Then
it screamed and went on through,
　　skewing as wrong the other way.

God damned it. This is hell,
   but I planned it, I sawed it,
I nailed it, and I
   will live in it until it kills me.
I can nail my left palm
   to the left-hand crosspiece but
I can't do everything myself.
   I need a hand to nail the right,
a help, a love, a you, a wife.

Man and Wife

ROBERT LOWELL
1917–1977

Tamed by Miltown, we lie on Mother's bed;
the rising sun in war paint dyes us red;
in broad daylight her gilded bed-posts shine,
abandoned, almost Dionysian.
At last the trees are green on Marlborough
    Street,
blossoms on our magnolia ignite
the morning with their murderous five days'
    white.
All night I've held your hand,
as if you had
a fourth time faced the kingdom of the mad—
its hackneyed speech, its homicidal eye—
and dragged me home alive. . . . Oh my *Petite*,
clearest of all God's creatures, still all air and
    nerve:
you were in your twenties, and I,
once hand on glass
and heart in mouth,
outdrank the Rahvs in the heat
of Greenwich Village, fainting at your feet—
too boiled and shy
and poker-faced to make a pass,

while the shrill verve
of your invective scorched the traditional South.

Now twelve years later, you turn your back.
Sleepless, you hold
your pillow to your hollows like a child,
your old-fashioned tirade—
loving, rapid, merciless—
breaks like the Atlantic Ocean on my head.

To His Wife

Decimus Magnus Ausonius
c. 310–c. 395

Be life what it has been, and let us hold,
Dear wife, the names we each gave each of old;
And let not time work change upon us two,
I still your boy, and still my sweetheart you.
What though I outlive Nestor? and what
   though
You in your turn a Sibyl's years should know?
Ne'er let us know old age or late or soon;
Count not the years, but take of each its boon.

TRANSLATED BY TERROT REAVELEY GLOVER

A Dedication

ALFRED, LORD TENNYSON
1809–1892

Dear, near and true—no truer Time himself
Can prove you, though he make you evermore
Dearer and nearer, as the rapid of life
Shoots to the fall—take this and pray that he
Who wrote it, honoring your sweet faith in
    him,
May trust himself; and after praise and scorn,
As one who feels the immeasurable world,
Attain the wise indifference of the wise;
And after Autumn past—if left to pass
His autumn into seeming-leafless days—
Draw toward the long frost and longest night,
Wearing his wisdom lightly, like the fruit
Which in our winter woodland looks a flower.

My Wife

ROBERT LOUIS STEVENSON
1850–1894

Trusty, dusky, vivid, true,
With eyes of gold and bramble-dew,
   Steel-true and blade-straight,
The great artificer
   Made my mate.

Honor, anger, valor, fire;
A love that life could never tire,
   Death quench or evil stir,
The mighty master
   Gave to her.

Teacher, tender, comrade, wife,
A fellow-farer true through life,
   Heart-whole and soul-free
The august father
   Gave to me.

To My More Than Meritorious Wife

JOHN WILMOT, EARL OF ROCHESTER
1647–1680

I am, by fate, slave to your will
And shall be most obedient still.
To show my love, I will compose ye,
For your fair finger's ring, a posy,
In which shall be expressed my duty,
And how I'll be forever true t'ye.
With low-made legs and sugared speeches,
Yielding to your fair bum the breeches,
I'll show myself, in all I can,
Your faithful, humble servant,

                    John.

A Dedication to My Wife

T. S. ELIOT
1888–1965

To whom I owe the leaping delight
That quickens my senses in our wakingtime
And the rhythm that governs the repose of our
    sleepingtime,
        The breathing in unison

Of lovers whose bodies smell of each other
Who think the same thoughts without need of
    speech
And babble the same speech without need of
    meaning.
No peevish winter wind shall chill
No sullen tropic sun shall wither
The roses in the rose-garden which is ours and
    ours only

But this dedication is for others to read:
These are private words addressed to you in
    public.

Poem in Prose

ARCHIBALD MACLEISH
1892–1982

This poem is for my wife.
I have made it plainly and honestly:
The mark is on it
Like the burl on the knife.

I have not made it for praise.
She has no more need for praise
Than summer has
Or the bright days.

In all that becomes a woman
Her words and her ways are beautiful:
Love's lovely duty,
The well-swept room.

Wherever she is there is sun
And time and a sweet air:
Peace is there,
Work done.

There are always curtains and flowers
And candles and baked bread
And a cloth spread
And a clean house.

Her voice when she sings is a voice
At dawn by a freshening sea
Where the wave leaps in the
wind and rejoices.

Wherever she is it is now.
It is here where the apples are:
Here in the stars,
In the quick hour.

The greatest and richest good,
My own life to live in,
This she has given me—

If giver could.

Part of Plenty

BERNARD SPENCER
1909–1963

When she carries food to the table and stoops
  down
—Doing this out of love—and lays soup with
  its good
Tickling smell, or fry winking from the fire
And I look up, perhaps from a book I am
  reading
Or other work: there is an importance of
  beauty
Which can't be accounted for by there and
  then,
And attacks me, but not separately from the
  welcome
Of the food, or the grace of her arms.

When she puts a sheaf of tulips in a jug
And pours in water and presses to one side
The upright stems and leaves that you hear
  creak,
Or loosens them, or holds them up to show me,
So that I see the tangle of their necks and cups
With the curls of her hair, and the body they
  are held

Against, and the stalk of the small waist rising
And flowering in the shape of breasts;

Whether in the bringing of the flowers or the
food
She offers plenty, and is part of plenty,
And whether I see her stooping, or leaning with
the flowers,
What she does is ages old, and she is not
simply,
No, but lovely in that way.

The Thinker

WILLIAM CARLOS WILLIAMS
1883–1963

My wife's new pink slippers
have gay pom-poms.
There is not a spot or a stain
on their satin toes or their sides.
All night they lie together
under her bed's edge.
Shivering I catch sight of them
and smile, in the morning.
Later I watch them
descending the stair,
hurrying through the doors
and round the table,
moving stiffly
with a shake of their gay pom-poms!
And I talk to them
in my secret mind
out of pure happiness.

While the Leaves of the Bamboo Rustle

ANONYMOUS FRONTIER GUARD
Eighth century

While the leaves of the bamboo rustle
On a cold and frosty night,
The seven layers of clobber I wear
Are not so warm, not so warm
As the body of my wife.

TRANSLATED BY GEOFFREY BOWNAS
AND ANTHONY THWAITE

The Shortest and Sweetest of Songs

GEORGE MACDONALD
1824–1905

Come
Home.

A Letter to Daphnis

ANNE, COUNTESS OF WINCHILSEA
1661–1720

This to the crown and blessing of my life,
The much loved husband of a happy wife;
To him whose constant passion found the art
To win a stubborn and ungrateful heart,
And to the world by tenderest proof discovers
They err, who say that husbands can't be
    lovers.
With such return of passion as is due,
Daphnis I love, Daphnis my thoughts pursue;
Daphnis my hopes and joys are bounded all in
    you.
Even I, for Daphnis' and my promise' sake,
What I in women censure, undertake.
But this from love, not vanity, proceeds;
You know who writes, and I who 'tis that reads.
Judge not my passion by my want of skill:
Many love well, though they express it ill;
And I your censure could with pleasure bear,
Would you but soon return, and speak it here.

To My Dear and Loving Husband

ANNE BRADSTREET
1612–1672

If ever two were one, then surely we.
If ever man were loved by wife, then thee;
If ever wife was happy in a man,
Compare with me, ye women, if you can.
I prize thy love more than whole mines of gold
Or all the riches that the East doth hold.
My love is such that rivers cannot quench,
Nor ought but love from thee, give recompense.
Thy love is such I can no way repay,
The heavens reward thee manifold, I pray.
Then while we live, in love let's so persevere
That when we live no more, we may live ever.

Any Wife or Husband

Carol Haynes

Let us be guests in one another's house
With deferential "No" and courteous "Yes";
Let us take care to hide our foolish moods
Behind a certain show of cheerfulness.

Let us avoid all sullen silences;
We should find fresh and sprightly things to
   say;
I must be fearful lest you find me dull,
And you must dread to bore me any way.

Let us knock gently at each other's heart,
Glad of a chance to look within—and yet
Let us remember that to force one's way
Is the unpardoned breach of etiquette.

So shall I be hostess—you, the host—
Until all need for entertainment ends;
We shall be lovers when the last door shuts,
But what is better still—we shall be friends.

I'm Wife . . .

EMILY DICKINSON
1830–1886

I'm wife; I've finished that,
That other state;
I'm Czar, I'm woman now:
It's safer so.

How odd the girl's life looks
Behind this soft eclipse!
I think that earth seems so
To those in heaven now.

This being comfort, then
That other kind was pain;
But why compare?
I'm wife! stop there!

The Shepherd's Wife's Song

ROBERT GREENE
1558–1592

Ah, what is love? It is a pretty thing,
As sweet unto a shepherd as a king;
    And sweeter too,
For kings have cares that wait upon a crown,
And cares can make the sweetest love to frown;
    Ah then, ah then,
If country loves such sweet desires do gain,
What lady would not love a shepherd swain?

His flocks are folded, he comes home at night,
As merry as a king in his delight;
    And merrier too,
For kings bethink them what the state require,
When shepherds careless carol by the fire:
    Ah then, ah then,
If country loves such sweet desires do gain,
What lady would not love a shepherd swain?

He kisseth first, then sits as blithe to eat
His cream and curds as doth the king his meat;
    And blither too,
For kings have often fears when they do sup,
Where shepherds dread no poison in their cup:
    Ah then, ah then,

If country loves such sweet desires do gain,
What lady would not love a shepherd swain?

To bed he goes, as wanton then, I ween,
As is a king in dalliance with a queen;
      More wanton too,
For kings have many griefs affects to move,
Where shepherds have no greater grief than
   love:
      Ah then, ah then,
If country loves such sweet desires do gain,
What lady would not love a shepherd swain?

Upon his couch of straw he sleeps as sound,
As doth the king upon his bed of down;
      More sounder too,
For cares cause kings full oft their sleep to spill,
Where weary shepherds lie and snort their fill:
      Ah then, ah then,
If country loves such sweet desires do gain,
What lady would not love a shepherd swain?

Thus with his wife he spends the year, as blithe
As doth the king at every tide or sithe;
      And blither too,
For kings have wars and broils to take in hand,
Where shepherds laugh and love upon the land:
      Ah then, ah then,
If country loves such sweet desires do gain,
What lady would not love a shepherd swain?

From The Song of Solomon

I am the rose of Sharon, and the lily of the valleys.

As the lily among thorns, so is my love among the daughters.

As the apple tree among the trees of the wood, so is my beloved among the sons. I sat down under his shadow with great delight, and his fruit was sweet to my taste.

He brought me to the banqueting house, and his banner over me was love.

Stay me with flagons, comfort me with apples: for I am sick of love.

His left hand is under my head, and his right hand doth embrace me.

I charge you, O ye daughters of Jerusalem, by the roes, and by the hinds of the field, that ye stir not up, nor awake my love, till he please.

The voice of my beloved! behold, he cometh leaping upon the mountains, skipping upon the hills.

My beloved is like a roe or a young hart: behold, he standeth behind our wall, he looketh forth at the windows, showing himself through the lattice.

My beloved spake, and said unto me, Rise up, my love, my fair one, and come away.

For, lo, the winter is past, the rain is over and gone;

The flowers appear on the earth; the time of the singing of birds is come, and the voice of the turtle is heard in our land:

The fig tree putteth forth her green figs, and the vines with the tender grape give a good smell. Arise, my love, my fair one, and come away.

O my dove, that art in the clefts of the rock, in the secret places of the stairs, let me see thy countenance, let me hear thy voice; for sweet is thy voice, and thy countenance is comely.

Take us the foxes, the little foxes, that spoil the vines: for our vines have tender grapes.

My beloved is mine, and I am his: he feedeth among the lilies.

Until the day break, and the shadows flee away, turn, my beloved, and be thou like a roe or a young hart upon the mountains of Bether.

West-running Brook

ROBERT FROST
1874–1963

"Fred, where is north?"
                        "North? North is there,
                        my love.
The brook runs west."
                        "West-running Brook then
                        call it."
(West-running Brook men call it to this day.)
"What does it think it's doing running west
When all the other country brooks flow east
To reach the ocean? It must be the brook
Can trust itself to go by contraries
The way I can with you—and you with me—
Because we're—we're—I don't know what we
    are.
What are we?"
                "Young or new?"
                            "We must be
                              something.
We've said we two. Let's change that to we
    three.
As you and I are married to each other,

We'll both be married to the brook. We'll build
Our bridge across it, and the bridge shall be
Our arm thrown over it asleep beside it.
Look, look, it's waving to us with a wave
To let us know it hears me."
                                "Why, my dear,
That wave's been standing off this jut of
    shore—"
(The black stream, catching on a sunken rock,
Flung backward on itself in one white wave,
And the white water rode the black forever,
Not gaining but not losing, like a bird
White feathers from the struggle of whose
    breast
Flecked the dark stream and flecked the darker
    pool
Below the point, and were at last driven
    wrinkled
In a white scarf against the far shore alders.)
"That wave's been standing off this jut of shore
Ever since rivers, I was going to say,
Were made in heaven. It wasn't waved to us."

"It wasn't, yet it was. If not to you
It was to me—in an annunciation."

"Oh, if you take it off to lady-land,
As't were the country of the Amazons
We men must see you to the confines of

And leave you there, ourselves forbid to
    enter,—
It is your brook! I have no more to say."

"Yes, you have, too. Go on. You thought of
    something."

"Speaking of contraries, see how the brook
In that white wave runs counter to itself.
It is from that in water we were from
Long, long before we were from any creature.
Here we, in our impatience of the steps,
Get back to the beginning of beginnings,
The stream of everything that runs away.
Some say existence like a Pirouot
And Pirouette, forever in one place,
Stands still and dances, but it runs away,
It seriously, sadly, runs away
To fill the abyss' void with emptiness.
It flows beside us in this water brook,
But it flows over us. It flows between us
To separate us for a panic moment.
It flows between us, over us, and *with* us.
And it is time, strength, tone, light, life, and
    love—
And even substance lapsing unsubstantial;
The universal cataract of death
That spends to nothingness—and unresisted,
Save by some strange resistance in itself,
Not just a swerving, but a throwing back,
As if regret were in it and were sacred.

It has this throwing backward on itself
So that the fall of most of it is always
Raising a little, sending up a little.
Our life runs down in sending up the clock.
The brook runs down in sending up our life.
The sun runs down in sending up the brook.
And there is something sending up the sun.
It is this backward motion toward the source,
Against the stream, that most we see ourselves
    in,
The tribute of the current to the source.
It is from this in nature we are from.
It is most us."
            "Today will be the day
You said so."
            "No, today will be the day
You said the brook was called West-running
    Brook."
"Today will be the day of what we both said."

Will You Love Me When I'm Old?

ANONYMOUS

I would ask of you, my darling,
    A question soft and low,
That gives me many a heartache
    As the moments come and go.

Your love I know is truthful,
    But truest love grows cold;
It is this that I would ask you:
    Will you love me when I'm old?

Life's morn will soon be waning,
    And its evening bells be tolled,
But my heart shall know no sadness,
    If you'll love me when I'm old.

Down the stream of life together
    We are sailing side by side,
Hoping some bright day to anchor
    Safe beyond the surging tide.
Today our sky is cloudless,
    But the night may clouds unfold;
But, though storms may gather round us,
    Will you love me when I'm old?

When my hair shall shade the snowdrift,
  And mine eyes shall dimmer grow,
I would lean upon some loved one,
  Through the valley as I go.
I would claim of you a promise,
  Worth to me a world of gold;
It is only this, my darling,
  That you'll love me when I'm old.

Oh, No—Not Ev'n When First We Lov'd

THOMAS MOORE
1779–1852

Oh, no—not ev'n when first we lov'd
   Wert thou as dear as now thou art;
Thy beauty then my senses mov'd,
   But now thy virtues bind my heart.
What was but Passion's sigh before
   Has since been turn'd to Reason's vow;
And, though I then might love thee *more*,
   Trust me, I love thee *better* now.

Although my heart in earlier youth
   Might kindle with more wild desire,
Believe me, it has gain'd in truth
   Much more than it has lost in fire.
The flame now warms my inmost core
   That then but sparkled o'er my brow,
And though I seem'd to love thee more,
   Yet, oh, I love thee better now.

The Marriage Ring

GEORGE CRABBE
1754–1832

The ring, so worn as you behold,
So thin, so pale, is yet of gold.
The passion such it was to prove:
Worn with life's care, love yet was love.

Constancy Rewarded

COVENTRY PATMORE
1823–1896

I vow'd unvarying faith, and she,
    To whom in full I pay that vow,
Rewards me with variety
    Which men who change can never know.

The Anniversary

JOHN DONNE
1572–1631

All Kings, and all their favourites,
    All glory of honours, beauties, wits,
The sun itself, which makes times, as they
    pass,
Is elder by a year now than it was
When thou and I first one another saw:
All other things to their destruction draw,
    Only our love hath no decay;
This no tomorrow hath, nor yesterday,
Running it never runs from us away,
But truly keeps his first, last, everlasting day.

    Two graves must hide thine and my corse;
    If one might, death were no divorce.
Alas, as well as other Princes, we
(Who Prince enough in one another be)
Must leave at last in death these eyes and
    ears,
Oft fed with true oaths, and with sweet salt
    tears;
    But souls where nothing dwells but love
(All other thoughts being inmates) then shall
    prove

This, or a love increasèd there above,
When bodies to their graves, souls from their
   graves remove.

   And then we shall be throughly blessed;
   But we no more than all the rest.
Here upon earth we're Kings, and none but
   we
Can be such Kings, nor of such subjects be;
Who is so safe as we? where none can do
Treason to us, except one of us two.
   True and false fears let us refrain,
   Let us love nobly, and live, and add again
   Years and years unto years, till we attain
To write threescore: this is the second of our
   reign.

To His Wife on the Fourteenth Anniversary of Her Wedding-Day, with a Ring

Samuel Bishop
1731–1795

"Thee, Mary, with this ring I wed,"
So fourteen years ago I said.
Behold another ring! "For what?"
To wed thee o'er again—why not?

With the first ring I married youth,
Grace, beauty, innocence, and truth;
Taste long admired, sense long revered,
And all my Molly then appeared.

If she, by merit since disclosed,
Prove twice the woman I supposed,
I plead that double merit now,
To justify a double vow.

Here then, to-day, with faith as sure,
With ardour as intense and pure,
As when amidst the rites divine
I took thy troth, and plighted mine,
To thee, sweet girl, my second ring,
A token and a pledge I bring;

With this I wed, till death us part,
Thy riper virtues to my heart;
Those virtues which, before untried,
The wife has added to the bride—
Those virtues, whose progressive claim,
Endearing wedlock's very name,
My soul enjoys, my song approves,
For conscience' sake as well as love's.

For why? They show me every hour
Honour's high thought, affection's power,
Discretion's deed, sound judgment's sentence,
And teach me all things—but repentance.

Story of the Gate

T. H. ROBERTSON

Across the pathway, myrtle-fringed,
Under the maple, it was hinged—
    The little wooden gate;
'T was there within the quiet gloam,
When I had strolled with Nelly home,
    I used to pause and wait

Before I said to her good-night,
Yet loath to leave the winsome sprite
    Within the garden's pale;
And there, the gate between us two,
We'd linger as all lovers do,
    And lean upon the rail.

And face to face, eyes close to eyes,
Hands meeting hands in feigned surprise,
    After a stealthy quest,—
So close I'd bend, ere she'd retreat,
That I'd grow drunken from the sweet
    Tuberose upon her breast.

We'd talk—in fitful style, I ween—
With many a meaning glance between
    The tender words and low;

We'd whisper some dear, sweet conceit,
Some idle gossip we'd repeat,
        And then I'd move to go.

"Good-night," I'd say; "good-night—good-bye!"
"Good-night"—from her with half a sigh—
        "Good-night!" "*Good*-night!" And then—
And then I do *not* go, but stand,
Again lean on the railing, and—
        Begin it all again.

Ah! that was many a day ago—
That pleasant summer-time—although
        The gate is standing yet;
A little cranky, it may be,
A little weather-worn—like me—
        Who never can forget

The happy—"End"? My cynic friend,
Pray save your sneers—there was no "end."
        Watch yonder chubby thing!
That is our youngest, hers and mine;
See how he climbs, his legs to twine
        About the gate and swing.

A Garden Song

George R. Sims
1847–1922

I scorn the doubts and cares that hurt
    The world and all its mockeries,
My only care is now to squirt
    The ferns among my rockeries.

In early youth and later life
    I've seen an up and seen a down,
And now I have a loving wife
    To help me peg verbena down.

Of joys that come to womankind
    The loom of fate doth weave her few,
But here are summer joys entwined
    And bound with golden feverfew,

I've learnt the lessons one and all
    With which the world its sermon stocks,
Now, heedless of a rise or fall,
    I've Brompton and I've German stocks.

In peace and quiet pass our days,
    With nought to vex our craniums,
Our middle beds are all ablaze
    With red and white geraniums.

And like a boy I laugh when she,
    In Varden hat and Varden hose,
Comes slyly up the lawn at me
    To squirt me with the garden hose.

Let him who'd have the peace he needs
    Give all his worldly mumming up,
Then dig a garden, plant the seeds,
    And watch the product coming up.

Two Lovers

George Eliot (Marian Evans)
1819–1880

Two lovers by a moss-grown spring:
They leaned soft cheeks together there,
Mingled the dark and sunny hair,
And heard the wooing thrushes sing.
    O budding time!
    O love's blest prime!

Two wedded from the portal stept:
The bells made happy carolings,
The air was soft as fanning wings,
White petals on the pathway slept.
    O pure-eyed bride!
    O tender pride!

Two faces o'er a cradle bent:
Two hands above the head were locked;
These pressed each other while they rocked,
Those watched a life that love had sent.
    O solemn hour!
    O hidden power!

Two parents by the evening fire:
The red light fell about their knees

On heads that rose by slow degrees
Like buds upon the lily spire.
O patient life!
O tender strife!

The two still sat together there,
The red light shone about their knees;
But all the heads by slow degrees
Had gone and left that lonely pair.
O voyage fast!
O vanished past!

The red light shone upon the floor
And made the space between them wide;
They drew their chairs up side by side,
Their pale cheeks joined, and said,
"Once more!"
O memories!
O past that is!

In Twos

WILLIAM CHANNING GANNETT

Somewhere in the world there hide
Garden-gates that no one sees
Save they come in happy twos,—
Not in one, nor yet in threes.

But from every maiden's door
Leads a pathway straight and true;
Map and survey know it not,—
He who finds, finds room for two!

Then they see the garden-gates!
Never skies so blue as theirs,
Never flowers so many-sweet,
As for those who come in pairs.

Round and round the alleys wind:
Now a cradle bars the way,
Now a little mound, behind,—
So the two go through the day.

When no nook in all the lanes
But has heard a song or sigh,
Lo! another garden-gate
Opens as the two go by.

In they wander, knowing not;
"Five and twenty!" fills the air
With a silvery echo low,
All about the startled pair.

Happier yet these garden-walks:
Closer, heart to heart, they lean;
Stiller, softer, falls the light;
Few the twos, and far between.

Till, at last, as on they pass
Down the paths so well they know,
Once again at hidden gates
Stand the two: they enter slow.

Golden Gates of "Fifty Years,"
May our two your latchet press!
Garden of the Sunset Land,
Hold their dearest happiness!

Then a quiet walk again:
Then a wicket in the wall:
Then one, stepping on alone,—
Then two at the Heart of All!

Inseparable

Philip Bourke Marston
1850–1887

When thou and I are dead, my dear,
  The earth above us lain;
When we no more in autumn hear
  The fall of leaves and rain,
Or round the snow-enshrouded year
  The midnight winds complain;

When we no more in green mid-spring,
  Its sights and sounds may mind,—
The warm wet leaves set quivering
  With touches of the wind,
The birds at morn, and birds that sing
  When day is left behind;

When, over all, the moonlight lies,
  Intensely bright and still;
When some meandering brooklet sighs
  At parting from its hill,
And scents from voiceless gardens rise,
  The peaceful air to fill;

When we no more through summer light
  The deep dim woods discern,
Nor hear the nightingales at night,
  In vehement singing, yearn

To stars and moon, that dumb and bright,
    In nightly vigil burn;

When smiles and hopes and joys and fears
    And words that lovers say,
And sighs of love, and passionate tears
    Are lost to us, for aye,—
What thing of all our love appears,
    In cold and coffined clay?

When all their kisses, sweet and close,
    Our lips shall quite forget;
When, where the day upon us rose,
    The day shall rise and set,
While we for love's sublime repose,
    Shall have not one regret,—

Oh, this true comfort is, I think,
    That, be death near or far,
When we have crossed the fatal brink,
    And found nor moon nor star,
We know not, when in death we sink,
    The lifeless things we are.

Yet one thought is, I deem, more kind,
    That when we sleep so well,
On memories that we leave behind
    When kindred souls shall dwell,
My name to thine in words they'll bind
    Of love inseparable.

"Till Death Us Part"

ARTHUR PENRHYN STANLEY
1815–1881

"Till death us part,"
Thus speaks the heart
When each to each repeats the words of doom;
For better and for worse,
Through blessing and through curse,
We shall be one, till life's last hour shall come.

Life with its myriad grasp
Our yearning souls shall clasp
By ceaseless love and still expectant wonder;
In bonds that shall endure
Indissolubly sure
Till God in death shall part our paths asunder.

Till death us join!
Oh, word yet more divine,
Which to the breaking heart breathes hope
  sublime!
Through wasted hours,
And shattered powers,
We still are one, despite the change and time.

Death with his healing hand
Shall knit once more the band,
Which needs but that one link that none may
sever;
Till, through the only Good,
Seen, felt, and understood,
The life in God shall make us one forever.

Epitaph on the Monument of
Sir William Dyer at Colmworth, 1641

LADY CATHERINE DYER

My dearest dust, could not thy hasty day
Afford thy drowsy patience leave to stay
One hour longer: so that we might either
Sit up, or gone to bed together?
But since thy finished labour hath possessed
Thy weary limbs with early rest,
Enjoy it sweetly: and thy widow bride
Shall soon repose her by thy slumbering side.
Whose business, now, is only to prepare
My nightly dress, and call to prayer:
Mine eyes wax heavy and the day grows old,
The dew falls thick, my blood grows cold.
Draw, draw closèd curtains: and make room:
My dear, my dearest dust; I come, I come.

An Epitaph Upon Husband and Wife Who Died and Were Buried Together

RICHARD CRASHAW
1612–1649

To these whom death again did wed
This grave's the second marriage-bed.
For though the hand of Fate could force
'Twixt soul and body a divorce,
It could not sever man and wife,
Because they both lived but one life.
Peace, good reader, do not weep;
Peace, the lovers are asleep.
They, sweet turtles, folded lie
In the last knot that love could tie.
Let them sleep, let them sleep on,
Till this stormy night be gone,
And the eternal morrow dawn;
Then the curtains will be drawn,
And they wake into a light
Whose day shall never die in night.

INDEX OF TITLES

INDEX OF POETS
AND TRANSLATORS